Spiritual Lives of the Great Composers

Other Books by Patrick Kavanaugh

Spiritual Moments with the Great Composers
Music of the Great Composers
Raising Musical Kids

Spiritual Lives of the Great Composers

Revised and Expanded

Patrick Kavanaugh

ZondervanPublishingHouse
Grand Rapids, Michigan

A Division of HarperCollinsPublishers

Spiritual Lives of the Great Composers
Copyright © 1992, 1996 by Patrick Kavanaugh

Requests for information should be addressed to:

⛪ ZondervanPublishingHouse
Grand Rapids, Michigan 49530

Library of Congress Cataloging-in-Publication Data

Kavanaugh, Patrick.
    [Spiritual lives of great composers]
    Spiritual lives of the great composers / Patrick Kavanaugh.
       p.   cm.
    Originally published as: The spiritual lives of great composers. Nashville, Tenn.:
Sparrow Press, c1992. With new introd.
    Includes bibliographical references (p.   ).
    ISBN 0-310-20806-8 (softcover)
    1. Composers—Religious life. 2. Religious life—Christianity. I. Title.
ML390.K23   1996
780'.92'2—dc20
[B]   96-2535
                                               CIP

Printed in the United States of America

---

97 98 99 00 01 02 /v DH/ 10 9 8 7 6 5

To my dear wife and best friend, Barbara

Contents

Acknowledgments

This book represents the work and support of more people than I could possibly hope to thank, but I cannot forgo mentioning the following:

The Directors of the Christian Performing Artists' Fellowship, Jim and Mary Jeane Kraft, Bob and Robin Sturm, Richard and Sherrill Lambert, Dennis and Jan Patrick, for their continued encouragement through the years of research, program notes, performances, and lectures.

Jennifer Rutherford, Jan Patrick, Wanda Skinner, Marthellen Hoffman, Connie Boltz, and Melanie Jeschke, for their excellent secretarial and artistic skills in preparing the manuscript.

The distinguished staff of the Library of Congress in Washington, D. C., for their assistance with original manuscripts, photographs, and research of the text.

Stan Gundry, Ann Spangler, and Mary McNeil of Zondervan Publishing for their enthusiastic support and commitment to excellence.

For the inspiration of my father, Edward J. Kavanaugh, the "other author" of the family.

I especially want to express gratitude to my wife, Barbara, and my wonderful children, Christopher, John, Peter, and David, for their infinite patience with a dad who stays up long into the night reading and typing.

Introduction

Music has such spiritual qualities that we should not be surprised at discovering the strong faith many composers possessed. Yet this is a subject that is seldom brought out in the biographies of great musicians or composers. Indeed, one can read about music and study music literature for years without ever being informed of the personal Christian beliefs that many of history's greatest musicians held.

This book, *The Spiritual Lives of Great Composers*, fulfills a tremendous need in the musical world. Its author, Dr. Patrick Kavanaugh, is a notable composer, conductor, lecturer, and Executive Director of the Christian Performing Artists' Fellowship. I have known Patrick for several years, and I am very enthusiastic about his dedication in faith, as well as his personal commitment to excellence. He has spent over five years of research at the Library of Congress in Washington, D.C., to bring together a inspiring chronicle of music's Christian heritage.

There is so much in this book that every musician needs to know. What a joy to find that so many of the great masterpieces we love were written to the glory of God. It strengthens our faith to see the higher purpose that motivated these composers, many of whom faced severe difficulties. Reading about them, we too may sense a mandate to follow the example of those who acknowledged that their talents were a gift from God.

I hope that as you read *The Spiritual Lives of Great Composers* you will be encouraged, as I have been, by the harmony of faith and giftedness that we have in the beauty of music.

Soli Deo Gloria!
Christopher Parkening

Preface

In this book, I have profiled twenty composers who come from a wide variety of backgrounds and beliefs. Yet among them there is a surprising level of agreement on basic Christian beliefs. Even men as dissimilar as Franz Joseph Haydn and Igor Stravinsky appear to hold in common an active spirituality.

This is not to imply that any of these composers lived the exemplary life of a saint. These were real human beings, often coping with very difficult circumstances and with their share of human failings. But each had a sincere faith. My purpose in writing this book is to focus on this often neglected aspect of their lives. Thus, this is a collection of the established, though little-known facts concerning the faith of twenty of the influential composers in our history.

Each chapter contains some biographical details to provide a background for the beliefs the different composers expressed. The essence of this writing, however, is not about what they *did*, but what they *believed*. There is already an abundance of excellent biographies on each of these composers. (See the notes and bibliography. In the volumes listed, readers can study all the typical details of the composers' careers and music.)

In the twentieth century, so much has been written about the negative side of composers' lives—anecdotes about their conceit, their tempers, their financial troubles, and their many failures—that a grossly inaccurate picture is often widely accepted without question. I wish to highlight verifiable aspects of these men's lives as they strove for good, sought to understand God, and found meaningful spiritual purpose in their lives.

Much of the material presented here is not emphasized in typical biographies. Instead, my material has been gathered largely from composers' letters and writings and recollections of these composers' friends and families. Extensive notes have been inserted to assist the reader in further research on the composers' beliefs.

The chapters conclude with some personal thoughts concerning a particularly striking characteristic of each composer's life—a characteristic that may have enabled them to achieve their respective places in history. All too often, studies on distinguished men become mere theoretical exercises. Few encourage the enrichment of the reader (and author). Therefore, these sections and the book's conclusion were written with the hope that readers may find inspiration, encouragement, and personal application. I have also provided a short section entitled "Recommended Listening" to assist those who may be new to the music of these composers and want to further explore the magnificence of their music.

This book has evolved from a number of experiences with the Christian Performing Artists' Fellowship (CPAF) with which I serve as the Executive Director. In the spring of 1989, CPAF was asked by the National Portrait Gallery to do a lecture-performance entitled "The Faith of the American Composer." In it, I included the material that appears here concerning Charles Ives and Igor Stravinsky. The following spring, CPAF sponsored several similar lecture-performances at Washington, D.C., universities entitled "The Spiritual Lives of Great Composers." For these events, I added the material on Bach, Mozart, Beethoven, and Wagner. The chapters on Handel, Haydn, Schubert, Mendelssohn, Liszt, and Dvořák were later researched for the program notes of certain CPAF performances. Finally, the eight new chapters on Chopin, Gounod, Franck, Bruckner, Brahms, Elgar, Vaughan Williams, and Messiaen were researched for Zondervan's expanded edition of this book.

Of course there are many more great masters than this book contains. The extensive research that goes into these articles will continue as part of the ongoing work of CPAF.

I hope this book will shed light on an important but so often overlooked subject of music history: the spiritual beliefs that underscore these composers' contributions to Western culture.

"Where there is devotional music, God is always at hand with His gracious presence."

Johann Sebastian
BACH

1685–1750

Through the autumn countryside of Germany, a young man of twenty walks briskly, soaking up the faded October sun and crunching fallen leaves underfoot. It is 1705, and the young man is on his way from Arnstadt to Lubeck—a two-hundred mile trek. The miles pass quickly as he anticipates the music he is determined to hear. One of the great organists of his day, Dietrich Buxtehude, will be performing evening musical devotions at the Cathedral this time of year, in preparation for Advent.

Traveling on foot to hear concerts was nothing new to this young organist; many times he had tramped thirty miles to Hamburg to hear the renowned organist Reincken and had even walked sixty miles to Celle to attend programs of French music. But to hear Buxtehude! For this opportunity, he needed at least a month's leave of absence from his position as a church organist. His superiors had grudgingly consented after the organist entreated them relentlessly for the necessary leave.

Arriving at Lubeck, footsore yet charged with excitement, the young musician drinks in the organ concerts of the master with a profound sense of personal inspiration. He sends word back to his employer at Arnstadt that he needs two months off instead of just one, knowing he risks being fired.

Three years after this experience, he announces his ultimate purpose in life: to create "well-regulated church music to the glory *of God." With an insatiable appetite to learn and a propensity for ceaseless work, he set about doing just that. His name was Johann Sebastian Bach.*

Throughout history, Bach has been acclaimed as the Christian composer, almost a kind of "patron saint" for church musicians. All around the world, he is recognized as one of the greatest composers in history. This is not to say there were no great spiritual composers before Bach; he actually represents the culmination of centuries of Christian music.

The sheer number of works he composed is staggering, however, and so is their diversity. They include chorales, cantatas, masses, oratorios, passions, concerti, and solo works for virtually every instrument of his day. Bach was prolific in other areas of life as well: He worked in a variety of demanding jobs (often with many extra-musical duties), and fathered twenty children, several of whom also matured into noted musicians.

When Johann Sebastian was born in 1685 in Eisenach, Germany, the Bach name was already synonymous with the musical trade. More than fifty musicians bearing that name are remembered by musicologists today. Even as a boy, Bach appeared eager to find expression for his emerging musical talent.

Orphaned at the age of nine, Johann moved in with an older brother, and his musical training began. He soon developed into an outstanding singer and demonstrated a remarkable ability to play the organ, the violin, and numerous other instruments. Bach's brother owned a set of compositions, which he forbade the younger Bach to use. Perhaps because it was placed off-limits, that musical manuscript grew irresistibly attractive to the young musician.

And so for weeks, Bach stole the precious pages and hid them in his room, where he stayed up late night after night copying the musical scores by moonlight. When his brother discovered the copied pages, he angrily confiscated them. But Bach had already gleaned valuable lessons in composition, as well as discipline and devotion to music, from the clandestine exercise.

Throughout his life he was known much more as an organist than as a composer. Amazing to us, only ten of Bach's original compositions were published during his lifetime. It was not until the nineteenth century that his brilliance as a composer was truly appreciated. Only then would he be revered by such masters as Beethoven, who claimed, "His name ought not to be Bach [*Bach* is the German word for *brook*], but ocean, because of his infinite and inexhaustible wealth of combinations and harmonies."

Like so many other masters throughout history, Bach's personality had many facets. On one hand, he was free from personal vanity and generous and encouraging toward his many pupils. The Bach family also had a great reputation for their hospitality. His first biographer, Forkel, notes, "These sociable virtues, together with his great artistic fame, caused his house to be rarely free from visitors."[1]

Once, when an acquaintance praised Bach's wonderful skill as an organist, he replied with characteristic humility and wit, "There is nothing very wonderful about it. You have only to hit the right notes at the right moment and the instrument does the rest."[2]

Yet he could be stubborn and irritable, especially with an unappreciative employer or an incompetent musician. At the age of twenty, Bach ridiculed a colleague by calling him "Kippelfagottist"—a "nanny-goat bassoonist." The offended musician picked up a stick and struck Bach, who drew his sword. A full-blown duel would have ensued, but fortunately, friends who saw the argument intensify threw themselves between the two adversaries to keep them apart.

Bach spent his entire life in Germany, working primarily as a church musician. For the two centuries prior, this region had been permeated by the legacy of Martin Luther, with his radical emphasis on a living, personal, Bible-based Christianity. Luther himself had been a musician, declaring music to be second only to the Gospel itself. Bach was to be the reformer's greatest musical disciple.

Bach resoundingly echoed the convictions of Luther, claiming that "Music's only purpose should be for the glory of God and the recreation of the human spirit."[3] As he set about composing, he would frequently initial his blank manuscript pages with the marking, "J. J." (*Jesu Juva*—"Help me, Jesus"),[4] or "I. N. J." (*In Nomine Jesu*—"In the name of Jesus").[5] At the manuscript's end, Bach routinely initialed the letters "S. D. G." (*Soli Deo Gloria*— "To God alone, the glory").[6] To Bach, these were not trite religious slogans but sincere expressions of personal devotion.

It is clear that Bach possessed a deep, personal, religious faith.[7] Indeed, it appears his entire life revolved around his spiritual convictions.[8] As one biographer has stated, "The focus of his emotional life was undoubtedly in religion, and in the service of religion through music."[9]

Bach's surviving letters also contain many references to his devout faith.[10] The love he felt for his large family is evident in a heartrending letter Bach wrote on behalf of an erring son who had incurred large debts and then left his town: "What can I do or say more, my warnings having failed, and my loving care and help having proved unavailing? I can only bear my cross in patience and commend my undutiful boy to God's mercy, never doubting that He will hear my sorrow-stricken prayer and in His good time bring my son to understand that the path of conversion leads to Him."[11]

His famous composer son, Carl Philipp Emanuel Bach, once claimed that the entire Bach family "were in the habit of beginning all things with religion."[12] Nothing in life, however mundane, was considered to be unspiritual. This is shown in a humorous poem Bach penned about his tobacco smoking, which ends with these words:

> "On land, on sea, at home, abroad,
> I smoke my pipe and worship God."[13]

In his spiritual outlook, Bach made no real distinction between sacred and secular music. For instance, at the beginning of such a "secular" work as his *Little Organ Book*, he wrote this dedication: "To God alone the praise be given for what's herein to man's use written."[14] His *Little Clavier Book*, like so many of his compositions, was inscribed "In the Name of Jesus."[15] Often, his compositions would contain chiastic structures, such as A B C D E D C B A. The visual equivalent of the resulting musical form appears as a cross.[16]

Bach was a master of "word painting," and used a large repertoire of musical devices to enhance the meaning of the text he was setting to music. Of the hundreds of examples of this technique, perhaps the best known is from his *St. Matthew Passion*. In this sublime work, Bach invokes a "divine halo" impression around the figure of Christ by having the strings play long, quiet tones whenever the lines of Jesus are sung. This continues without exception until Jesus' line from the cross, "My God, my God, why have you forsaken me?" At this crucial moment, when Christ's humanity is supreme, the halo of strings is removed, and the emotional effect is unforgettable.

Another memorable scene is found in his colossal *Mass in B Minor*. Toward the end of the dramatic "Crucifixus" movement, the voices and instruments quietly sink into their lowest registers as the body of Jesus is musically lowered into the tomb. This is immediately followed by an explosion of blazing glory in the "Et Resurrexit," an effect composers have copied for centuries.

Even humor was skillfully used when Bach set the Scriptures to music. In his *Magnificat*, as Bach was setting the Latin words of "He has filled the hungry with good things, but the rich he has sent away empty," he had a clever idea. To depict the word *inanes* (empty), he has the flutes abruptly stop playing and leaves but one note in the continuo to fill up the emptiness of the last bar of music! Surely he could not resist a smile as he added this touch to his masterpiece.

As a sincere Lutheran, Bach was a devoted reader of the Bible and other religious volumes. His personal library contained eighty-three books, inventoried at his death. All of them explored spiritual matters. Besides the Bible, there were two different editions of Martin Luther's collected works and dozens of books by Luther's disciples and champions of the seventeenth and eighteenth centuries.[17]

Bach sought spiritual connections between his faith and his art. Even in the midst of study, his pen was rarely still. He inserted a marginal note in his biblical commentary on 1 Chronicles 25, in which King David sets apart musicians for the temple worship: "This chapter is the true foundation for all God-pleasing music."[18] At the conclusion of 1 Chronicles, he noted, "Splendid proof that . . . music was instituted by the Spirit of God through David."[19]

Another of the composer's favorite passages must have been 2 Chronicles 5:13, describing a temple worship service in ancient Israel with these words: "The trumpeters and singers joined in unison, as with one voice, to give praise and thanks to the Lord. . . . Then the temple of the Lord was filled with a cloud, and the priests could not perform their service . . . for the glory of the Lord filled the temple of God." As Bach paused to contemplate these verses, he wrote in the margin of his commentary, "Where there is devotional music, God is always at hand with His gracious presence."[20]

A religious controversy in Bach's day was touched off by a movement known as Pietism. The fervency of this antiritual group appealed to Bach, who held other doctrines in common with it, including a deep mysticism,[21] and an almost passionate longing for death.[22] But the Pietists were incorrigible "art haters," calling the church cantata a "sinful abomination."[23] Bach could never align himself with a movement that he considered at odds with the biblical view of music.

Bach was, from first to last, a church musician. At the height of his fame, he left the only secular position he ever held, Capellmeister of the court of Prince Leopold. He chose instead an obscure position as Cantor at a church in Leipzig, where he would again be cloistered in his unacclaimed but beloved world of church music.

Bach's eyes began failing toward the end of his life, and by age sixty-five he was completely blind. He died in relative obscurity in 1750, and his grave was not even marked.[24] His last work, dictated from his bed, was a chorale entitled *Before Thy Throne I Come*.[25]

Some Thoughts on Bach: Productivity

Bach's musical genius stands as a marvel through more than two centuries since his death. Yet the musician did not believe that he was singled out for unsurpassed genius. He told a student, "Just practice diligently, and it will go very well. You have five fingers on each hand just as healthy as mine."

When asked the secret of his genius, he answered simply, "I was made to work; if you are equally industrious you will be equally successful." It is doubtful whether anyone in the world of music has matched Bach's industriousness. When his multitudinous scores were finally collected and published, the job took the Bach Gesellschaft forty-six years, and the completed edition filled sixty huge volumes.

Yet all of his composing took place while Bach was fulfilling dozens of other tasks: working as an organist, a conductor, a music director, a private instructor, even a teacher of Latin to young boys—not to mention raising a large family and moving from post to post. The inspiration and beauty of his music are abundantly apparent. Yet the real mystery of Bach's life as a composer concerns how he found the actual time to write it all, and still more, to have created so many masterpieces cherished through the ages.

Bach personified the German Protestant work ethic. "I was made to work" could have been his life motto. Yet he was never known to speak a word of complaint. On the contrary, he seems to have reveled in his decades of musical toil, dating from the time he copied forbidden compositions at night. And even in his final year of life, after an operation left him sightless, Bach worked frantically to revise his great choral fantasies.

Bach's devotion to God and his drive to express that devotion musically gave the world a gift for all to appreciate. His productivity forged a musical legacy that Richard Wagner would someday appraise as "the most stupendous miracle in all music."

Recommended Listening

Orchestral Music: 6 Brandenburg concerti; 4 suites

Keyboard music: *The Well-Tempered Clavier*; *Goldberg Variations*; 6 French suites; 6 English suites; 6 partitas

Organ Music: *Toccata and Fugue in D Minor*

Choral Music: *The Passion According to St. Matthew*; *Mass in B Minor*; *Magnificat*; *Christmas Oratorio*; *Easter Oratorio*; church cantatas, notably no. 4 ("Christ lag in Todesbanden"), no. 80 ("Ein' feste Burg ist unser Gott"), and no. 140 ("Wachet Auf")

> "It pleased the Almighty, to whose great Holy Will I submit myself with Christian submission."

George Frédéric
HANDEL

1685–1759

In a small London house on Brook Street, a servant sighs with resignation as he arranges a tray full of food he assumes will not be eaten. For more than a week, he has faithfully continued to wait on his employer, an eccentric composer, who spends hour after hour isolated in his own room. Morning, noon, and evening the servant delivers appealing meals to the composer and returns later to find the bowls and platters largely untouched.

Once again, he steels himself to go through the same routine, muttering under his breath about how oddly temperamental musicians can be. As he swings open the door to the composer's room, the servant stops in his tracks.

The startled composer, tears streaming down his face, turns to his servant and cries out, "I did think I did see all Heaven before me, and the great God Himself." George Frédéric Handel had just finished writing a movement that would take its place in history as the Hallelujah Chorus.

If Handel's father had had his way, the *Hallelujah Chorus* would never have been written. His father was a "surgeon-barber"—a no-nonsense, practical man who was determined to send his son to law school. Even though young Handel showed extraordinary musical talent as a child, his father refused for several years to permit him to take lessons.

George Frédéric was born in 1685, a contemporary of Bach, a fellow German, and was raised a fellow Lutheran, yet they were never to meet. Though numerous books on the lives of great composers begin with Bach, Handel, in fact, was born several weeks earlier, on February 23, 1685.

When the boy was eight or nine years old, a duke heard him play an organ postlude following a worship service. Handel's father was summarily requested to provide formal music training for the boy. By the time Handel turned twelve, he had written his first composition and was so proficient at the organ that he substituted, on occasion, for his own teacher.

Young Handel continued to master the clavichord, oboe, and violin, as well as composition through the years. In 1702 he entered the University of Halle to study law out of respect for his late father's desire. But he soon abandoned his legal studies and devoted himself entirely to music.

He became a violinist and composer in a Hamburg opera theater, then traveled to Italy, where he lived from 1706 to 1710 under the patronage of their music-loving courts. In Rome, he wrote *The Resurrection*, an oratorio in which religious themes emerged for the first time in Handel's music. While in Italy, Handel met some of the eminent musicians of his day, most notably Domenico Scarlatti.

In 1712, after a short stay at the court of Hanover, he moved to England, where he lived for the rest of his life. There he anglicized his name from its original spelling, Georg Friedrich. He dropped the diaeresis originally on the "a" of his surname, and this led to various spellings by different publishers: Haendel, Hendel, and so on.

Handel was the sort of individual who stands out in a crowd. Large-boned and loud, he often wore an enormous white wig with curls cascading to his shoulders. When he spoke, his English was replete with colorful snatches of German, French, and Italian.

Although Handel wrote his greatest music in England, he suffered personal setbacks there as well. Falling in and out of favor with changing monarchs, competing with established English composers, and dealing with fickle, hard-to-please audiences left him confronting bankruptcy more than once.

Yet Handel retained his sense of humor through virtually any hardship. Once, just as an oratorio of his was about to begin, several of his friends gathered to console him about the extremely sparse audience attracted to the performance. "Never mind," Handel joked to his friends. "The music will sound the better" due to the improved acoustics of a very empty concert hall!

Like his fellow composer Bach, Handel was also renowned as a virtuoso organist. One Sunday, after attending worship services at a country church, Handel asked the organist's permission to play a postlude. As the congregation was leaving the church, Handel began to play with such expertise that the people reclaimed their seats and refused to withdraw. The regular organist finally stopped him, saying that Handel had better not play the postlude after all, if the people were ever to go home.

Audiences for Handel's compositions were unpredictable, and even the Church of England attacked him for what they considered his notorious practice of writing biblical dramas such as *Esther* and *Israel in Egypt* to be performed in secular theaters. His occasional commercial successes soon met with financial disaster, as rival opera companies competed for the ticket holders of London. He drove himself relentlessly to recover from one failure after another, and finally his health began to fail. By 1741 he was swimming in debt. It seemed certain he would land in debtor's prison.

On April 8 of that year, he gave what he considered his farewell concert. Miserably discouraged, he felt forced to retire from public activities at the age of fifty-six. Then two unforeseen events converged to change his life. A wealthy friend, Charles Jennens, gave Handel a libretto based on the life of Christ, taken entirely from the Bible.[1] He also received a commission from a Dublin charity to compose a work for a benefit performance.

Handel set to work composing on August 22 in his little house on Brook Street in London.[2] He grew so absorbed in the work that he rarely left his room, hardly stopping to eat. Within six days part one was complete. In nine days more he had finished part two, and in another six, part three. The orchestration was completed in another two days.[3] In all, 260 pages of manuscript were filled in the remarkably short time of 24 days.

Sir Newman Flower, one of Handel's many biographers, summed up the consensus of history: "Considering the immensity of the work, and the short time involved, it will remain, perhaps forever, the greatest feat in the whole history of music composition."[4] Handel's title for the commissioned work was, simply, *Messiah*.

Handel never left his house for those three weeks.[5] A friend who visited him as he composed found him sobbing with intense emotion.[6] Later, as Handel groped for words to describe what he had experienced, he quoted St. Paul, saying, "Whether I was in the body or out of my body when I wrote it I know not."[7]

Messiah premiered on April 13, 1742, as a charitable benefit, raising 400£ and freeing 142 men from debtor's prison.[8] A year later, Handel staged it in London. Controversy emanating from the Church of England continued to plague Handel,[9] yet the King of England attended the performance. As the first notes of the triumphant *Hallelujah Chorus* rang out, the king rose. Following royal protocol, the entire audience stood too, initiating a tradition that has lasted for more than two centuries.

Soon after this, Handel's fortunes began to increase dramatically, and his hard-won popularity remained constant until his death. By the end of his long life, *Messiah* was firmly established in the standard repertoire. Its influence on other composers would be extraordinary. When Haydn later heard the *Hallelujah Chorus*, he wept like a child, and exclaimed, "He is the master of us all!"

Handel personally conducted more than thirty performances of *Messiah*. Many of these concerts were benefits for the Foundling Hospital, of which Handel was a major benefactor.[10] The thousands of pounds that Handel's performances of *Messiah* raised for charity led one biographer to note: "*Messiah* has fed the hungry, clothed the naked, fostered the orphan . . . more than any other single musical production in this or any country."[11] Another wrote, "Perhaps the works of no other composer have so largely contributed to the relief of human suffering."[12]

This work has had an uncanny spiritual impact on the lives of its listeners. One writer has stated that *Messiah*'s music and message "has probably done more to convince thousands of mankind that there is a God about us than all the theological works ever written."[13]

The composer's own assessment, more than any other, may best capture his personal aspirations for his well-loved work. Following the first London performance of *Messiah*, Lord Kinnoul congratulated Handel on the excellent "entertainment." Handel replied, "My lord, I should be sorry if I only entertain them. I wish to make them better."[14]

The religious beliefs of the composer who created the world's most popular religious masterpiece have puzzled many musicologists. In an era when Christian musicians typically worked for local churches, this composer of secular opera and chamber and orchestral music did not fit the usual pattern. Yet he was a devout follower of Christ and widely known for his concern for others.[15] Handel's morals were above reproach.[16] At church he was often seen "on his knees, expressing by his looks and gesticulations the utmost fervor of devotion."[17]

Yet the very persistence that kept Handel going through the worst of times made him obstinate and temperamental when he encountered opposition. A confirmed bachelor, Handel was reputed to swear in several languages when moved to wrath (usually by singers). At the same time, he was equally quick to admit his own fault and apologize.

Handel was known for his modest and straightforward opinion of himself and his talent. When a friend unwittingly commented on the dreariness of some music he had heard at the Vauxhall Gardens, Handel rejoined, "You are right, sir, it is pretty poor stuff. I thought so myself when I wrote it."

His friend Sir John Hawkins recorded that Handel "throughout his life manifested a deep sense of religion. In conversation he would frequently declare the pleasure he felt in setting the Scriptures to music, and how contemplating the many sublime passages in the Psalms had contributed to his edification."[18] In one of his few surviving letters, Handel comforts his brother-in-law on the death of Handel's mother: "It pleased the Almighty, to whose great Holy Will I submit myself with Christian submission."[19]

Known universally for his generosity and concern for those who suffered, Handel donated freely to charities even in times when he faced personal financial ruin. He was a relentless optimist whose faith in God sustained him through every difficulty. Raised as a sincere Lutheran, he harbored no sectarian animosities and steered clear of denominational disagreements.[20] Once, defending himself before a quarrelsome archbishop, Handel simply replied, "I have read my Bible very well, and will choose for myself."[21]

A few days before Handel died, he expressed his desire to die on Good Friday, "in the hopes of meeting his good God, his sweet Lord and Savior, on the day of his Resurrection."[22] He lived until the morning of Good Saturday, April 14, 1759. His death came only eight days after his final performance, at which he had conducted his masterpiece, *Messiah*.

His close friend James Smyth wrote, "He died as he lived—a good Christian, with a true sense of his duty to God and to man, and in perfect charity with all the world."[23] Handel was buried in Westminster Abbey, with over three thousand in attendance at his funeral.[24] A statue erected there shows him holding the manuscript for the solo that opens part three of *Messiah*, "I know that my Redeemer liveth."[25]

Some Thoughts on Handel: Resilience

When reviewing the lives of great figures in history, it is tempting to focus only on the end results of their lives, glossing over the periods between the masterpieces they produced. Because "the end of the story" is a matter of record, it may be difficult to appreciate the struggles that threatened to make the story far shorter. In Handel's case especially, had he not possessed an amazing ability to bounce back from repeated disaster, such well-loved works as *Messiah* and the *Royal Fireworks Music* would have never been written.

How often Handel must have felt like giving up! What fits of depression his many failures would have caused an average composer. To a man who knew he had but one great talent, seeing that talent go unrewarded so often must have been profoundly perplexing. And to see other London composers, whom he knew to have less genius, enjoying the success that eluded him for so many years—must have driven Handel to extreme exasperation. Yet through all the frustrating years before his final successes, Handel simply refused to quit.

And, as if blows inflicted by his competitors were not painful enough, Handel suffered from an onslaught of attacks within his own camp. For a devoted Christian to have come under censure by the principal church of his time must have been bitterly distressing. Even after *Messiah* was becoming well known, as great a religious figure as John Newton (composer of the hymn "Amazing Grace"), preached every Sunday for over a year against the "secular" performances of this biblical oratorio. Yet Handel did not respond by counterattacking his Anglican brothers. Though he remained a Lutheran, he "would often speak of it as one of the great felicities of his life that he was settled in a country where no man suffers any molestation or inconvenience on account of his religious principles."

Handel refused to be deterred by setbacks, attacks, illnesses, or even severe financial woes. It is a tribute to the faith and optimism Handel possessed, relying on God as he worked to overcome significant obstacles and to create music that is universally cherished today.

Recommended Listening

Orchestral Music: 12 concerti grossi; *Water Music*; *Royal Fireworks Music*

Chamber Music: 6 sonatas for recorder; 8 sonatas for violin

Keyboard: *Suite in D Minor*; *Chaconne in G*

Oratorio: *Messiah*; *Israel in Egypt*; *Judas Maccabaeus*; *Esther*

"Since God
has given me
a cheerful
heart, He will
forgive me for
serving Him
cheerfully."

Franz Joseph
HAYDN

1732–1809

The prince is enjoying himself immensely. He spent eleven million florins to build his magnificent castle and estate in the countryside near Vienna, and he indulged his new home with every conceivable luxury. And now, relaxed and surrounded by his treasures, Prince Paul Esterhazy listens to his private orchestra perform a new symphony.

He gazes at the musicians he retains year-round and congratulates himself on having recently put them in their place. How dare they complain, *the prince muses,* and ask for more time off to visit their families? After all, I treat them just like family right here. . . .

The prince's reverie is broken all at once when two of the musicians stop playing, snuff out the candles on their music stands, and walk off the stage. Wait! What is going on here? *The prince inhales loudly. As he watches, two more musicians, and then two more make their exits as well. The prince jumps to his feet, perplexed, and turns his attention to the conductor, who seems singularly unruffled by these abrupt departures.*

Prince Esterhazy slowly takes his seat again as the light of understanding dawns. What had the conductor called this new symphony he composed? *the prince wondered.* Oh yes, the Farewell. *Finally, only two violins are left, and the conductor himself begins gathering up his score and preparing to leave.*

By now the prince has taken the hint. Before his conductor leaves the room, the prince stops him. He now gives his approval to the musicians' demand for extra leave time. The prince's music director and conductor, Franz Joseph Haydn, had made his point.

Haydn, one of the most successful and famous composers in history, came from the most humble surroundings. He was born in the small town of Rohrau, in lower Austria, to parents who loved music but were quite poor. They recognized Haydn's musical talent when he was very young, and at age six he was sent to a nearby town for musical training. Two years later he became a choirboy in Vienna, and for the next nine years he sang in the famed St. Stephen's Cathedral in Vienna.

When his voice began changing in 1749, his secure life as a choirboy ended. He was dismissed from the cathedral and soon found himself, at age seventeen, miserable and penniless. Haydn lived hand to mouth by giving lessons and playing the violin for Vienna serenades.

Haydn had been raised a Roman Catholic, and later in life he frequently expressed gratitude to his parents for "bringing him up in the fear of God."[1] His parents urged Haydn to become a priest,[2] and at one point he agreed to enter the Servite order.[3] But he concluded that God's call on his life did not require him to enter the priesthood; instead, it meant training and exercising his prodigious musical talents. One day he wrote, "I know that God has favored me, and recognize it thankfully. I also believe that I have done my duty and have been of use to the world through my works. Let others do the same!"[4]

In the eighteenth century, there were few concert halls and public performances in Vienna. The best way for a musician to make a living outside the church was to be hired by a rich nobleman. It took time, but Haydn finally made contact with important musicians of his day. His first regular job was as music director for the court of Count Morzin.

Then in 1761, the turning point in Haydn's life came when he was hired by Prince Paul Esterhazy. Moving to the Prince's grand country estate marked the beginning of nearly three decades during which Haydn would spend his musical life in the finest circumstances a composer could desire.

While he was employed by the Esterhazy nobility, Haydn produced an enormous amount of music. He would complete 104 symphonies, 76 string quartets, masses, oratorio, opera, concerti, and dozens of chamber works. It is no wonder he has become known among music historians as the "Father of the Symphony," the "Father of the String Quartet," and even the "Father of the Sonata."

For Haydn, music brought unparalleled purpose and joy to life. In contrast, his home life was a source of pain and unfulfilled promise. As a young man, he fell in love with a girl who later stunned him by entering a convent. Impulsively, he proposed to her older sister, and she agreed to marry him. The two newlyweds proved utterly incompatible. Haydn's new bride had so little regard for his composing genius that she cut up his manuscripts to use for hair-curling papers!

Eventually they agreed to a separation. Nonetheless, Haydn remained faithful, never considering divorce. He generously supported his wife throughout his life and in his will. He is remembered never to have spoken an unkind word about her.

Haydn's disappointing attempt at marriage did not deter his zest for composing or hinder his deep faith in God. In many ways, his work and his faith were intricately linked. In the morning, Haydn awakened early and prayed on his knees daily, before beginning to compose.[5]

Seated at his clavier, Haydn searched for an idea, a theme, an image to set to music. "If it soon comes without much difficulty, it expands," Haydn once said. "But if it does not make progress, I try to find out if I have erred in some way or other, thereby forfeiting grace; and I pray for mercy until I feel that I am forgiven."[6]

In recalling his struggles while composing a certain sacred work, Haydn wrote, "I prayed to God—not like a miserable sinner in despair—but calmly, slowly. In this I felt that an infinite God would surely have mercy on his finite creature, pardoning dust for being dust. These thoughts cheered me up. I experienced a sure joy so confident that as I wished to express the words of the prayer, I could not express my joy, but gave vent to my happy spirits and wrote above the Miserere, 'Allegro.'"[7]

His music is so ebullient in temperament that it was actually criticized by more puritanical members of the church. Haydn's reply was characteristic: "Since God has given me a cheerful heart, He will forgive me for serving him cheerfully."[8]

When Haydn pondered the reality of a God who cared for him, and for all people, he said his heart "leapt for joy."[9] He could not prevent his music from expressing the same exuberance— even when the music was conveying one of Christianity's more somber themes.

Once, as he was setting to music the familiar words from the Mass: Agnus Dei, qui tollis peccata mundi ("Lamb of God, who takes away the sins of the world"), Haydn said he was seized by an "uncontrollable gladness."[10] He even had to apologize to Empress Marie Therese on this point, explaining that the certainty of God's grace had made him so happy that he wrote a joyful melody to accompany the sober words.[11]

It was always his goal, he said, to "depict Divinity through love and goodness."[12] One of Haydn's many sacred works, the Stabat Mater, was among his favorites because it had been composed to fulfill a religious vow made after recovering from a serious illness.[13]

Like Bach before him, Haydn began most of his scores with the words, In Nomini Jesu,[14] and ended them with Laus Deo or Soli Deo Gloria.[15] His close friend, Georg August Griesinger, said that Haydn was "loyally devoted to the faith in which he was raised. He was strongly convinced in his heart that all human destiny was under God's guiding hand, that God rewards the good and the evil, and that all talents come from above."[16]

Haydn's unique combination of faith and work may have achieved its culmination with his oratorio, The Creation, finished at the age of sixty-six. The Creation was written to inspire "the adoration and worship of the Creator," Haydn wrote, and to put the listener "in a frame of mind where he is most susceptible to the kindness and omnipotence of the Creator."[17]

Haydn later recalled, "Never was I so devout as when I composed *The Creation*. I knelt down each day to pray to God to give me strength for my work."[18] He told a friend, "When I was working on *The Creation* I felt so impregnated with the Divine certainty, that before sitting down to the piano, I would quietly and confidently pray to God to grant me the talent that was needed to praise him worthily."[19]

Haydn was a faithful Catholic, yet his life and his music were nonsectarian. A Protestant clergyman who knew him wrote that Haydn "appeared to me to be a religious character, and not only attentive to the forms and usages of his church, but under the influence of a devotional spirit." This man, the Reverend C. J. Latrobe, considered Haydn "his spiritual father."[20] Though the composer knew the Mass by heart,[21] at least once he even changed Catholic texts to place a greater emphasis on Christ.[22]

At the urging of his devoted friend, Mozart, Haydn once joined the Order of Freemasons in Vienna.[23] His interest in this group waned quickly, and he never attended any of their secret meetings.[24] His life and music were for all the world. He told a group of musicians who banded together to play his *Creation*, "There are so few happy and contented people here below, sorrow and anxiety pursue them from everywhere; perhaps your work may, some day, become a spring from which the careworn may draw a few moment's rest and refreshment."[25]

Haydn always insisted that his talents were an unmerited gift from God. "Our Almighty Father had endowed me with so much faculty in music that even in my sixth year I stood up like a man and sang Masses in the church choir," he once reminisced.[26] In an autobiographical sketch, he concluded, "I offer all my praises to Almighty God, for I owe them to Him alone; my sole wish is to neither offend my neighbor, nor my gracious Prince, nor above all our merciful God."[27]

Toward the end of his productive life, Haydn's faith increased in fervor. He approached death calmly, telling his friend Griesinger, "I only have to wait like a child for the time when God calls me to Himself."[28] As an old man, he gave the following advice to the Vienna choirboys, "Be good and industrious and serve God continually."[29]

He also kept his humor to the end. In 1805, a rumor spread that Haydn had died. Many composers wrote memorial pieces, and in Paris a special concert was arranged, including Mozart's Requiem. When Haydn found out about his widely rumored death, he sent a letter thanking the musicians for their well-meant gestures. He added, "Had I only known of it in time, I could have traveled to Paris to conduct the Requiem myself!"

Joseph Haydn died peacefully in 1809, soon after Napoleon occupied Vienna. Showing deep regard for the composer's universal celebrity, this conquering enemy of Austria placed an honor guard at Haydn's home and assigned his highest officers to Haydn's funeral. His will—which generously remembered people whom he had not seen for decades—began, "In the Name of the Most Holy Trinity," and continued, "My soul I bequeath to its all-bountiful Creator."[30]

The last performance Haydn attended was *The Creation*, on March 27, 1808. As the music ended and the audience applauded enthusiastically, Haydn lifted his hands toward heaven and said, "Not from me—from there, above, comes everything."[31]

Some Thoughts on Haydn: Humility

By the time Haydn died, he had become recognized as the greatest living composer. From the most insignificant of beginnings he achieved universal acclaim, and from a childhood of poverty he worked his way into considerable wealth. Yet throughout his long climb, he remained the same modest and reserved man who had played for his supper on the streets of Vienna.

Once, late in life, when Haydn met a devotee who heaped praise upon him, Haydn cut him off. "Do not speak so to me. You see only a man whom God has granted talent and a good heart." Never ashamed of his humble upbringing, he would often go to church in his shirt-sleeves, like a peasant. In the class-conscious society in which he spent his entire adult life, how refreshing it must have been to be with a self-made genius whose ego did not grow with his fortune.

Perhaps the secret to Haydn's humility lay in the unassuming contentment he displayed in all circumstances. Long before his later prosperity, he told a friend, "When I sit at my old worm-eaten piano, I envy no king in his happiness." The simplicity of this great genius was sincere. When he grew old, he said, "I have associated with kings, emperors, and many great gentlemen and have heard many flattering things from them; but I do not wish to live on an intimate footing with such persons, and I prefer people of my own status."

Haydn simply refused to be lured by the trappings of the world. He was content with what he had, and he made a habit of expressing thanks to God and to those around him. Without complaint, he remained accessible to the musicians who worked under him and often presented their needs to their common employer. Even when the king of England, George III, complimented Haydn on the great deal of music he had created, the reply was simply, "Yes, Sire, a great deal more than is good." Long after his fame was established, Haydn all but disdained his wages, given by the Prince to his "undeserving self." In Haydn's case, this was not a mere expression of servility but an outgrowth of his true attitude of mind.

Without this humility, his climb to success and wealth might have resulted in much less music for posterity to enjoy. He could have rested on past laurels, retired early, and enjoyed the good life. Instead, he chose to work almost to the very end of his life, living unpretentiously and giving generously to others. Haydn composed some of his finest masterpieces in his sixties and seventies, including *The Creation*, *The Seasons*, and *The Seven Last Words of Christ*.

Recommended Listening

Orchestral Music: 104 symphonies, notably no. 45 ("Farewell") and no. 94 ("Surprise")

Chamber Music: 83 string quartets, notably op. 76, no. 3 ("The Emperor") and op. 76, no. 4 ("Sunrise")

Piano Music: 52 piano sonatas, notably no. 49 ("Genzinger")

Oratorio: *The Creation; The Seasons*

Choral Music: *The Lord Nelson Mass; Mass in Time of War*

"God is ever before my eyes. I realize His omnipotence and I fear His anger; but I also recognize His love, His compassion, and His tenderness towards His creatures."

Wolfgang Amadeus
MOZART

1756–1791

*The Papal Choir excelled during its Holy Week perfor-
mances, leaving the worshipers breathless in reverent praise. In
one pew, a young boy visiting the Vatican leans forward expec-
tantly, transported by the music.*

*He listens intently as the choir sings its annual presentation
of a beloved Miserere, a composition protected by papal decree.
By law, this work could not be performed elsewhere, and the only
manuscript of the music was closely guarded by the Vatican. Anyone who attempted to copy it would be punished immediately by
excommunication.*

*After the performance, the young Austrian lad settles down
at a desk in his room and writes out—from memory—every note
of the elaborate Miserere he had just heard. News of this facsim-
ile makes its way back to the Pope, and the Vatican buzzes with
speculation over what would happen next.*

*The boy's punishment? Instead of excommunicating the boy
for his feat of phenomenal genius, the Pope presents young Wolfgang Amadeus Mozart with a select Vatican honor: the coveted
Cross of the Order of the Golden Spur.*

The very term "child prodigy" seems to bear a special affinity
for Johann Chrysostom Wolfgang Amadeus Mozart, born in
Salzburg, Austria, in 1756. At age three he amused himself at the

keyboard. At four his formal training began, and within a year he was improvising minuets. When he turned six, his loving but ambitious father arranged the first of many concert tours in which little Wolfgang performed for the delighted courts and nobility of Europe.

An advertisement for one of Mozart's child performances drew crowds of curious bystanders: "He will play a concerto on the violin, and will accompany symphonies on the harpsichord—the keyboard being covered with a cloth—with as much facility as if he could see the keys.

"He will instantly name all the notes played at a distance, whether singly or in chords, on the harpsichord or on any other instrument, bell, glass, or clock. He will finally improvise as long as may be desired, and in any key, on the harpsichord and the organ."

As he matured, Mozart's reputation as a composer soon rivaled his fame at the keyboard. He produced an avalanche of compositions: symphonies, operas, chamber music, concerti, masses, and songs, all of which seemed to flow effortlessly from his pen. He would generally work out the details of his composition in his head, and later write down the notes in astonishing time. His barber even complained about the difficulty of dressing Mozart's hair—the composer would constantly be getting an idea and dash to the keyboard, with the barber in hot pursuit. Explaining his enormous artistic energy, Mozart answered simply, "Composition is less tiring than doing nothing."[1]

Mozart's genius attracted attention throughout Europe. It produced a number of jealous rivals who did their best to discredit him. But it also won him many friends, notably the great Haydn from Esterhazy. After hearing several of Mozart's string quartets, Haydn exclaimed to the composer's proud father, "I assure you before God, as an honorable man, your son is the greatest composer that I know personally or by reputation." These beautiful quartets Mozart later dedicated to his "caro amico Haydn."

Mozart was also perceptive in recognizing the talent of others. When a brash, young, and unknown musician named Beethoven insisted on playing for the celebrated Mozart, the latter was very impressed. He turned to his friends nearby and uttered a prophetic remark: "Keep your eyes on him. Someday he will give the world something to talk about." Years later, Beethoven would return the compliment, writing in 1826, "I have always reckoned myself among the greatest venerators of Mozart, and I shall remain so until my last breath."

The spiritual life of this great Austrian composer has often been overlooked. Despite notorious portrayals by a few modern writers and movie makers, the true picture of the man emerges from his personal letters—and hundreds have been preserved—from recollections of those who knew him, and from the work of serious musicologists. Mozart possessed an unusual, multifaceted personality that bears little resemblance to contemporary caricatures of him.

Mozart remained childlike throughout his short life. Carefree and confident, he loved games, dancing, and masque balls. He had almost no financial sense, which led to disaster when money was scarce, but this was partly born out of his intrinsic generosity. When a fellow composer's illness kept him from fulfilling a commission and endangered his salary, Mozart completed the work by his friend's bedside, taking no credit for its composition. At another time, Mozart was accosted by a beggar in the streets of Vienna. Having no money to give, he brought the man to a coffeehouse, quickly wrote down an entire minuet and trio, gave them to the man with a letter, and sent him to his publisher. The astonished panhandler soon possessed five guineas.

For the most part, Mozart's life reflects a moral reputation and a steadfast faith in God. Friedrich Kerst, one of the editors of the composer's published letters, states, "Mozart was of a deeply religious nature. . . . Mozart stood toward God in a relationship of a child full of trust in his father."[2]

Mozart's parents were pious Catholics, and their son developed a sincere, personal relationship to Christ. Mozart's faith stayed intact even when he came under attack by corrupt churchmen. The most notorious example of this was the heartless

Archbishop of Salzburg, who belittled Mozart, impaired his career, and one day had the musician physically tossed out of his cathedral.

Most of Mozart's correspondence is lighthearted and witty, and it is true that one set of letters written to a young cousin sinks to indecency. But this is the rare exception, though it has been popularly capitalized upon.

One of the dozens of letters the composer wrote to his father details his sensitivity to spiritual matters and his reliance on God: "Papa must not worry, for God is ever before my eyes. I realize His omnipotence and I fear His anger; but I also recognize His love, His compassion, and His tenderness towards His creatures. He will never forsake His own. If it is according to His will, so let it be according to mine. Thus all will be well and I must needs be happy and contented."[3]

Concerning his personal morals, Mozart writes, "I cannot possibly live like the majority of our young men. In the first place, I have too much religion, in the second too much love for my fellow men and too great a sense of honor . . . "[4] He assured his worrisome father that, "I know that I have so much religion that I shall never be able to do a thing which I would not be willing openly to do before the whole world."[5] He once canceled a tour with two musicians of ill-repute, noting that, "Friends who have no religion are not stable."[6]

As a fourteen-year-old, Mozart reported that he prayed every day, and he wrote requests for prayer from Christians around him.[7] Even some of his compositions, such as the great *Mass in C Major*[8] and the *Davidde Penitente*,[9] were the result of sacred vows he had made privately with God.

Prayer accompanied a major part of Mozart's life. When his father expressed concern over Mozart's upcoming marriage, Mozart answered that he and Constanze shared a unique spiritual compatibility. He insisted, "I found that I never prayed so heartily, confessed or communicated so devoutly, as when by her side. And she feels the same."[10]

The Mozarts had a loving and steadfast marriage, strong enough to withstand the attacks aimed at them by Mozart's critics in Vienna. Scandalous tales of Mozart's womanizing have long since been discounted. Constanze, although as financially inept as her husband, was a faithful helpmate to Mozart as he worked.

On many late nights, Mozart would pore frantically over his musical scores by candlelight, while Constanze attended him. She prepared his favorite punch and amused him with stories and jokes while he composed, to help him stay awake.

Toward the end of his life, Mozart joined a Freemason lodge in Vienna. It should be noted that modern Masonic institutions have evolved considerably from those social gatherings of the eighteenth century, which included such members as Samuel Wesley and George Washington.[11] Katherine Thomson, in her inclusive study of the Masonry of that period, insisted that for Mozart it was certainly not "inconsistent for a Freemason to be a Christian."[12] The musicologist Alfred Einstein even suggested that Mozart's attraction to Masonry was primarily for social reasons. He wrote that, "Perhaps he was driven into the Lodge by his feeling of profound loneliness as an artist and his need for unreserved friendship."[13]

Mozart's faith was deeply personal. It bore the marks of Roman Catholicism, Protestant influence, eighteenth-century-Enlightenment thinking, and the Freemason movement, yet it was authentically Christian. His true faith was based on a private relationship between himself and Christ.

Mozart's letters are often punctuated with expressions of faith and praise to God, as well as concern for the spiritual lives of those around him: "It will greatly assist such happiness as I may have to hear that my dear father and my dear sister have submitted wholly to the will of God, with resignation and fortitude—and have put their whole confidence in Him, in the firm assurance that He orders all things for the best."[14]

While hoping to receive an appointment from Elector Karl Theodore in 1777, Mozart wrote, "Let come what will, nothing can go ill as it is the will of God; and that it may so go is my daily prayer."[15] The following year, he tells of the success of a new symphony: "I prayed to God for His mercy that all might go well, to His greater glory, and the symphony began."[16]

When a friend was seriously ill, Mozart comforted his mother and sister: "You should not grieve too deeply, for God's will is always the best. God will know whether it is better to be in this world or the other."[17] After the composer's beloved mother died, he wrote, "By a singular grace of God I endured all with steadfastness and composure. When her illness grew dangerous, I prayed God for two things only—a happy hour of death for my mother, and strength and courage for myself. God heard me in His loving kindness, heard my prayer and bestowed the two mercies in largest measure."[18]

His faith concerning the issues of life and death shows strong conviction. "I believe, and nothing shall ever persuade me differently, that no doctor, no man, no accident, can either give life to man or take it away; it rest with God alone."[19]

At age thirty-one, Mozart may already have had premonitions about the brevity of his own life. His reflections, at this age, indicate a mature Christian commitment: "I never lie down in my bed without reflecting that perhaps I—young as I am—may not live to see another day; yet none of all who know me can say that I am socially melancholy or morose. For this blessing I daily thank my Creator and wish it from my heart for all my fellow men."[20]

Just four years later, at age thirty-five, Mozart died. His health, which had always been frail, at last failed him while he worked in poverty on his last great masterpiece, the Requiem.

His biographer, Otto Jaun, has summarized the consensus of history, when he calls Mozart's Requiem, "The truest and most genuine expression of his nature as an artist. It is his imperishable monument."[21] A contemporary of Mozart writes, "Mozart has disclosed his whole inner being in this one sacred work, and who can fail to be affected by the fervor of devotion and holy transport which streams from it? His Requiem is unquestionably the highest and best that modern art has to offer for sacred worship."[22] The composer's expressive treatment of the centuries-old Latin text clearly reveals his strong faith in "The Lamb of God, who takes away the sins of the world."

At one point, Mozart confessed to Constanze that he believed death was near and that he was writing Requiem for himself.[23] Racked with pain on his deathbed, and surrounded by several friends, the composer sang the alto part at an informal rehearsal of the unfinished work. During the "Lacrimosa" movement, Mozart burst into tears, and his final rehearsal ended.[24] He died early the next morning, December 5, 1791. His last action was to imitate the kettledrums in his Requiem.

Mozart left behind not only an unparalleled legacy of musical treasure but a record of eighteenth-century faith. A genius such as Mozart possessed, developed so fully in so young a man, may have tempted others to spiritual indifference. Mozart leaves evidence of a different response. He wrote in a letter, "Let us put our trust in God and console ourselves with the thought that all is well, if it is in accordance with the will of the Almighty, as He knows best what is profitable and beneficial to our temporal happiness and our eternal salvation."[25]

Some Thoughts on Mozart: Enthusiasm

It has often been said that the difference between a successful man and a failure is not the number of problems each may have but the fact that the successful man takes action to overcome his problems. Mozart was a man of action and enthusiasm. The many volumes of his compositions show us that he spent his thirty-five years achieving, not content to sit and rest on the laurels of a childhood career.

Mozart was a sensation as a prodigy, yet as a man he was surrounded by depressing misfortunes. The very genius that could have resulted in success caused intense jealousy among rival composers, some of whom openly worked for Mozart's ruin. He was never given the well-paid position that he obviously deserved. His last decade was a continual struggle against poverty for himself and his dearly beloved family. If he had been inclined to discouragement, he had enough affliction to completely paralyze his musical output.

Yet his response was the very opposite of paralysis. When the pressures of money mismanagement were overpowering him, Mozart would tear headlong into a brilliant new composition. When he saw other composers winning the public and denouncing his works, he would begin anew, writing innovative works that would eventually eclipse his competitors' best efforts. A lesser man might have allowed his bitter predicaments to stifle his imagination, but Mozart sustained his enthusiastic drive even through the debilitating suffering of his last year.

Ultimately, generations have received the benefit of thousands of Mozart's works because he simply refused to be a slave to the circumstances around him. When he obtained a commission, he quickly fulfilled the request. But even when he went without such an incentive, he continued to create masterpieces, such as his last great symphonies, composed without commission or even the prospect of an upcoming performance.

The stupendous number of his compositions proves that action is the best remedy for discouragement. As long as he could compose, he was incapable of despair. His indefatigable spirit— which was cultivated as a successful prodigy—had taught him to find his motivation internally, with or without the impetus of praise from others.

Recommended Listening

Orchestral Music: 41 symphonies, notably no. 40 in G Minor and no. 41 in C Major, ("Jupiter"); *Eine kleine Nachtmusik* for strings

Chamber Music: 23 string quartets, notably the 6 "Haydn" quartets; 2 piano quartets; *Quintet in A Major* for clarinet and strings

Keyboard: 21 piano sonatas, notably *Sonata in A Major*, K. 331

Choral Music: *Requiem; Ave Verum Corpus*

Operas: *The Marriage of Figaro; Don Giovanni; The Magic Flute*

"In whatsoever manner it be, let me turn to Thee and become fruitful in good works."

Ludwig van
BEETHOVEN

1770–1827

An opera rehearsal is under way, and the singers and orchestra members focus closely on their conductor. He gestures wildly as the musicians struggle to interpret his intent. What could he possibly want them to do? Two violinists exchange furtive glances, commiserating wordlessly about how difficult it is to work with such an idiosyncratic composer and conductor.

The music deteriorates into a cacophony of random notes, then falls helplessly silent. Yet the conductor seems confused, obviously unaware of the reason for the rehearsal's breakdown. The sight of this man's horrified face points toward only one conclusion, the musicians gradually realize. He is deaf, and he is trying valiantly to conceal his deafness.

Who will put a stop to this travesty? The embarrassed musicians shift awkwardly in their chairs, staring at their instruments or at one another and not daring to look at the conductor. The conductor scrutinizes the instruments in the laps of the musicians and studies their mortified faces. He summons a friend to his side, and the friend scribbles a note: "Please do not go on; more at home."

The conductor reads the note hastily, then turns on his heel and races out of the opera hall. He does not stop running until he reaches his home, where he throws himself on the sofa and buries his face in his hands. For hours, Ludwig van Beethoven remains in a devastating state of depression, no longer able to hide the loss of his hearing from the world.

Ludwig van Beethoven, considered by many the greatest composer who ever lived, was a devoted admirer of Handel and his music. On his deathbed, he claimed, "Handel is the greatest, cleverest composer. From him I can still learn." It is no wonder that Beethoven felt a special kinship with his predecessor; both men continued their artistic endeavors in the face of great adversity. Handel struggled against an intermittent series of external misfortunes, however, while Beethoven's conflict was internal.

From the time he was born in 1770, Beethoven faced overwhelmingly difficult circumstances. His alcoholic father proved irresponsible and harsh, and his loving mother remained frail and sickly until her death at age forty. Beethoven's talent for music presented itself when he was a young boy, yet his father was not successful at exploiting it in the same way as Mozart's father.

When he was a young man, Beethoven moved to Vienna, the musical capital of Europe, and began performing for the nobles who gathered there. His virtuosity at the piano made him extremely popular with the aristocracy, even when his crude manners left them aghast. Beethoven's mannerisms and general appearance were notoriously rough and clumsy, yet he was not the least bit intimidated by his refined patrons. He made no attempt to impress them or to change his uncultured ways.

A disheveled Beethoven frequently took long walks in the countryside. Once, at the height of his fame, a police officer mistook him for a tramp as he wandered outside the city of Baden. Placing him under arrest, the officer must have smiled indulgently in disbelief as Beethoven loudly protested, indignantly declaring his identity. He would have spent the night in jail, but a local musician came to his rescue, identifying the unkempt derelict as the great Beethoven.

Beethoven matured at a time when all of Europe was in an uproar. Revolution was in the air, all forms of establishment were being challenged, and Napoleon was on the march, relentlessly conquering every nation in his path. At first, Beethoven admired the might of this new conqueror and planned to dedicate his third symphony to him. But when he learned that Napoleon had proclaimed himself Emperor, Beethoven flew into a rage and tore up the title page. The composer's stormy life is marked by many such outbursts, triggered by events large and small. Once, at a restaurant, a waiter mistakenly brought him the wrong order. An enraged Beethoven hurled the dish and food into the very face of the flustered servant.

He had many devoted friends, yet Beethoven's life was characterized by loneliness and misunderstanding. He remained a bachelor, though not by choice. He proposed to several different women, all of whom admired his genius but clearly perceived that his erratic personality would make him an intolerable husband.

The defining tragedy of his life, and the one that diminished his performing career, was his growing deafness. The pain and humiliation he experienced because of it drove him almost to suicide. In 1802, he poured out his heart in a letter to his brothers, saying that deafness meant he "must live as an exile."[1]

Beethoven wrote, "It was impossible to say to others: 'Speak louder; shout! For I am deaf.' . . . How great was the humiliation when one who stood beside me heard the distant sound of a shepherd's pipe, and I heard nothing—or heard the shepherd sing, and I heard nothing. Such experiences brought me to the verge of despair."[2]

It was this miserable affliction, and not malice toward others, that intensified the tumultuous eruption of emotion that is found throughout Beethoven's life and music. A friend once watched in anguish while the former master pianist attempted to play piano in a rehearsal of his Archduke Trio. It turned out to be one of the last times Beethoven ever played his instrument for anyone. After hearing the pathetic attempt, Beethoven's friend wrote, "If it is a great misfortune for any one to be deaf, how can a musician endure it without giving way to despair? Beethoven's continual melancholy was no longer a riddle to me."[3]

In his famous Heiligenstadt Testament, the deaf composer gave voice to his deepest longings: "Almighty God, you look down into my innermost soul, you see into my heart and you know that it is filled with love for humanity and a desire to do good."[4]

Indeed, Beethoven could be altruistic and sympathetic to the affliction of others. When he learned that Bach's only remaining daughter was in need, he immediately offered to publish a new work for the elderly woman's exclusive benefit.

As Beethoven's deafness increased, he withdrew more and more into the work of composing and into his intimate and unorthodox relationship to God. Beethoven lived until 1827. On his deathbed he reassured his brother of his "great readiness" to make his peace with God.[5] One of the last acts of his life was to receive Communion.[6] Beethoven's friend, Anselm Huttenbrenner, remained with the composer at his death, which took place during a violent storm. Following a loud clap of thunder, Huttenbrenner wrote, the unconscious Beethoven awoke, "opened his eyes, raised his right hand, his fist clenched, and looked upward for several seconds with a grave, threatening countenance, as if to say, 'I defy you, powers of evil! Away! God is with me!'"[7]

Discerning Beethoven's beliefs is no easy task. All of his biographers agree that he was intensely spiritual,[8] and his close friend, Anton Felix Schinder, insists that Beethoven's "entire life is proof that he was truly religious at heart."[9] But his untraditional faith makes it difficult to categorize the composer.[10] Beethoven, like many geniuses, was a very complex man with eclectic interests and influences.

Beethoven was born and baptized into a Roman Catholic family. His mother, it is reported, was very pious, and young Beethoven was sent to a Catholic school. There, as he commented later, he was brought up "with proverbs" by a Jesuit teacher.[11] In his youth he attended a variety of churches, and his principal teacher and mentor, Christian Gottlob Neefe, was a Protestant believer.[12]

Beethoven's diaries, letters, and conversation books (with which he communicated after he was deaf) contain dozens of devout references to God, giving evidence of strong conviction. In a typical spirit of forceful certitude, he wrote, "It was not a fortuitous meeting of chordal atoms that made the world. If order and beauty are reflected in the constitution of the universe, then there is a God."[13]

His relationship to God was deeply personal, and he turned to God to make sense out of life's unfairness: "Therefore, calmly will I submit myself to all inconsistency and will place all my confidence in your eternal goodness, O God! My soul shall rejoice in Thee, immutable Being. Be my rock, my light, forever my trust!"[14] In 1815, he even expressed his hope of finding tranquility and fulfillment in composing for "a small chapel" where he would dedicate his works to "the glory of God, the Eternal."[15]

Throughout his diary, ardent prayers appear:[16] "In whatsoever manner it be, let me turn to Thee and become fruitful in good works."[17] To a close friend in 1810, he confessed an almost childlike faith. He wrote, "I have no friend. I must live by myself. I know, however, that God is nearer to me than others. I go without fear to Him, I have constantly recognized and understood Him."[18] To his friend, the Grand Duke Rudolf, Beethoven wrote, "Nothing higher exists than to approach God more than other people and from that to extend His glory among humanity."[19]

Beethoven owned both a French and a Latin Bible[20] and, at least late in life, he prayed with his young nephew every morning and evening.[21] His library included such Christian devotionals as Thomas à Kempis' *The Imitation of Christ* [22] and a very heavily marked copy of Christian Sturm's *Reflections on the Works of God in Nature*, the work of a Lutheran minister.[23] "Socrates and Jesus have been my models,"[24] Beethoven wrote in a conversation book of 1820. His devotion was simple and private. In a letter to a friend, he commented, "Today happens to be Sunday, so I will quote you something out of the Bible, 'See that ye love one another.'"[25]

And of course, Beethoven composed some of the most profound Christian masterpieces of history. The most notable of these include his oratorio *Christ on the Mount of Olives*,[26] which seems to embody Beethoven's identification with the suffering Savior; the *Mass in C*, which Beethoven termed "especially close to my heart";[27] and his monumental *Missa Solemnis*, considered by many to be the greatest mass ever composed. His *Gellent Songs*, op. 48, were settings of religious poems, prayers, and a psalm. These were not commissioned but were freely chosen by the composer because of his affinity for their spiritual texts.[28]

Beethoven's spiritual convictions show themselves even in his musical sketches. In the manuscript of his *String Quartet no. 15*, he writes, "Song of Thanksgiving to God on the recovery from an illness, in the Lydian Mode."[29] In the sketches of the *Pastoral Symphony*, he wrote, "Oh Lord, we thank thee."[30] For years Beethoven showed a preoccupation with the church modes. In 1809 he wrote, "In the old church modes the devotion is divine . . . and God let me express it someday."[31] He contemplated composing a choral symphony, describing it as "a pious song in a symphony, in the old modes; Lord God, we praise thee, alleluia."[32]

Nevertheless, other aspects of his life seem to contradict this picture. Although Beethoven was born a Roman Catholic, he never practiced this faith.[33] He had a marked suspicion of priests and avoided going to church.[34] His brash personality seemed, outwardly at least, to prevent Christian charity from being recognized. Beethoven had a strong interest in Eastern literature, and he even copied three Hindu passages that he kept under glass on his desk.[35] He had no scruples whatsoever in quoting pagan verse, such as the famous "daughter of Elysium" from the Ninth Symphony. "Elysium" originated as a pagan name for heaven.[36] That Beethoven believed in the Christian religion cannot seriously be doubted, but his personal faith embraced idiosyncratic interpretations that go well beyond the rituals of the typical churchgoer.[37]

Beethoven's complex personality traits leave the world's greatest musicologists at odds on the subject of the composer's faith. Perhaps the best clues to his personal beliefs can be found in Beethoven's music—music that reveals the man himself. Evidence of Beethoven's serious, searching approach to matters of faith may be found in his greatest sacred work, *Missa Solemnis*. For this composition, Beethoven took unprecedented pains with his research, studying the history of church music, gathering hymn manuscripts from local monasteries,[38] even obtaining a new and more accurate translation of the Latin so every word would be fully understood.[39]

He wrote at the top of the score, "From the heart—may it go to the heart."[40] Possibly the cornerstone of *Missa Solemnis* is the movement "Dona nobis pacem," over which he inscribed, "A prayer for inner and outer peace."[41] This is the peace that Beethoven sought all his life and found, it would seem, if only at his death.

Some Thoughts on Beethoven: Determination

The portrait of Beethoven's life that emerges from historical accounts, his own written reflections, and his music is one of tremendous achievement in the face of unimaginable difficulty and tragedy. He confronted a physical affliction that not only was constant and worsening, but one that caused him shame, humiliation, and disgrace. Yet he refused to succumb to the dejection created by his deafness. Year after silent year he continued to compose masterpieces that actually increased, rather than abated, in musical excellence.

Today, in a world marked by medical and technological advances as well as public awareness and acceptance of physical defects, it is difficult to grasp the devastating nature of the obstacles Beethoven faced. Now there are unobtrusive and effective hearing aids, worn with no more thought of shame than a common pair of glasses. But if Beethoven wanted to hear at all, he had to hold up a bulky, cumbersome ear trumpet. This not only exposed his abnormality to everyone around him but also attracted the catcalls of street urchins and delinquents in Vienna.

Hearing loss such as this would present a severe trial to anyone, but for a musician—indeed, a master musician—deafness was devastating. Beethoven wrote, "Alas! How could I possibly refer to the impairing of a sense which in me should have been more perfectly developed than in other people, a sense which at one time I possessed in the greatest perfection, even to a degree of perfection such as few in my profession possess or have ever possessed—oh, I cannot do it."

Nevertheless, Beethoven was determined to prevail and to continue in his art, which he considered a sacred trust placed upon him by his Creator. The very strength and resolve that piqued others to call him brusque and tactless enabled him to continue and even to expand his natural compositional gifts. It is astonishing to study the complexities and beauty of his late works and to realize that, except in his imagination, he never heard them performed.

Beethoven's principal virtue was his sheer determination to overcome, although this often obscured the many other virtues he possessed. The judgment of a man's greatness is not only to be measured in the mission he accomplishes but in the obstacles he has overcome in the process. Not only was the genius of this deaf eccentric recognized by his contemporaries, thousands of whom lined the streets of Vienna at his funeral, but also in the universal veneration of every subsequent musical age.

Recommended Listening

Orchestral Music: 9 symphonies, notably no. 3 ("Eroica"), no. 5, no. 6 ("Pastoral"), and no. 9 ("Choral"); 5 concerti for piano, notably no. 55 ("Emperor"); *Concerto for Violin*

Chamber Music: 16 string quartets, notably no. 14 in C-sharp Minor

Piano Music: 32 piano sonatas, notably no. 8 ("Pathetique") and no. 14 ("Moonlight")

Choral Music: *Missa Solemnis; Mass in C; Christ on the Mount of Olives*

Opera: *Fidelio*

"It sometimes
seems to me
as if I did not
belong to this
world at all."

Franz Peter
SCHUBERT

1797–1828

Seeking some diversion from his work, the young composer stops in at a favorite Vienna café. It's a bit shabby, but caters to a fascinating variety of artists and vagabonds. As his eyes adjust to the dim candlelight, he makes his way toward a group of friends gathered at a small table and settles down comfortably among them. He digs into his pockets and finds there is not enough money for a glass of wine. He contents himself with a cup of coffee.

To take his mind off pressing thoughts of unpaid debts and poor health, the composer thumbs through a German edition of Shakespeare's Cymbeline. The lively chatter of his friends begins to quiet as they notice the gleam in the composer's eye. He reads aloud the words of a poem in the Shakespeare play that begins, "Hark, hark, the lark." A lovely melody comes to mind, and the composer insists he must write it down.

But the café is quite dark, and there is no paper. One of his friends grabs a menu and scratches down some staves on the back of it. The composer sets to work, scribbling rapidly in the dim light. Within moments, his work is completely finished.

That evening the composer, Franz Peter Schubert, and his friends gather around the piano. His new composition, one of the most beautiful songs of the nineteenth century, is performed for the first time.

The short life of Franz Schubert is a study in incongruity. Known for so many beautiful and joyful compositions, he encountered a doleful succession of disappointments, anguish, and poverty. Born in Vienna to a penniless schoolmaster and his wife, Schubert never received a thorough musical education. His talents were so abundant, however, that in 1808, at age eleven, he was accepted as a chorister in the court chapel. A few years later he began to compose. He persevered even when he was so poor he could not afford music paper; the only paper he owned for composing was given as a gift.

When his voice broke in 1813, Schubert (like Haydn sixty-four years earlier), was abruptly dismissed from the court chapel. Discouraged and disheartened, he worked for three joyless years in his father's school. Then he embraced an unconventional, happy-go-lucky existence and stayed with it for the rest of his life. Fortunately, his cheerful disposition won him a great number of friends, some of whom formed a musical clique called the Schubertians. These were not rich patrons who could solve his financial problems, but they did encourage him to compose many of his greatest masterpieces.

Schubert spent most of his life destitute and struggling, but financial hardship never diminished his enthusiasm to compose. It is astonishing to see how many hundreds of compositions came pouring out of his imagination—songs, symphonies, chamber music, masses, and piano works—dozens of which are considered standard repertoire today. He stated, "When one piece is finished, I begin another." Schubert even went to bed with his glasses on so he could begin working as soon as he awoke!

Sadly, his music brought the composer almost no income whatsoever. In 1823, his remarkable song, *The Erl-King*, became very popular and finally secured him considerable earnings, but he carelessly sold the rights to this classic for the equivalent of a few hundred dollars. He sold a publisher twelve volumes of his songs for 800 florins; from just one of these, the *Wanderer*, the publisher profited over 36,000 florins.

Another time, Schubert completed two orchestra movements and sketched two more, then he dropped the project and sent the manuscript away. One of his friends retrieved this score in 1865, and as a result, Schubert's *Unfinished Symphony* was finally premiered. It continues to be one of the most celebrated musical fragments in history.

Personal tragedy compounded Schubert's difficulties, particularly after he befriended a young man named Franz Schober. Removed from his father's guiding influence, Schubert was, in the words of other friends, "led astray" by this irreligious man. Few details remain of their escapades in the Vienna nightlife, but most scholars today believe Schubert contracted syphilis as a result.

Theatre managers continually refused to stage Schubert's operas, and the relentless strain of rejection darkened the composer's optimistic temperament. He worked occasionally for the family of Count Esterhazy, but most of the local music posts he desired and felt he deserved went to other composers.

Schubert's great hero was Beethoven. Although they had scarcely met, Beethoven had studied some of his songs and proclaimed, "Truly in Schubert dwells a divine spark!" The younger composer deeply grieved when his hero died, and he carried a torch in Beethoven's funeral procession. Within two years Schubert himself lay dying, in a delirious fever diagnosed as typhus, the common disease of the city slums. He was only thirty-one years old.

Schubert's short life passed in relative obscurity, and many details about his thoughts and beliefs remain unknown. Yet it is evident that his personal faith in God served to strengthen his spirits against oppressive hard times. His close friend Anselm Huttenbrenner wrote, "Schubert had a devout nature and believed firmly in God and the immortality of the soul. His religious sense is also clearly expressed in many of his songs. At the time when he was in want, he in no way lost courage, and if, at times, he had more than he needed he willingly shared it with others who appealed to him for alms."[1]

Schubert's baptismal certificate affirms that his parents were both "believers in the Catholic religion,"[2] and they appeared to be particularly devout. A young friend once reminisced about Schubert's consideration toward others, saying it "showed that his mother had laid the foundation of religious feeling and uprightness with great care and motherly tenderness, filling his youthful heart with these."[3]

His father's faith is evident in a consoling letter he wrote to his other son, soon after the composer's untimely death. In it, the father exhorts him to "seek comfort in God, and to bear any affliction that may fall on us according to God's wise dispensation with resolute submission to His holy will. And what befalls us shall convince us of God's wisdom and goodness, and give us tranquillity. Therefore take courage and trust implicitly in God. He will give you strength, that you may not succumb, and will grant you a glad future by His blessing."[4]

Schubert's education, if musically inadequate, at least encouraged his spiritual growth. When he joined the chapel choir, he gained admittance to the Imperial and Royal City Seminary and consequently to its clerical lectures.[5] Biographers note that when his old music teacher Papa Holzer encouraged Franz to write him some church music, "the boy did not need much urging."[6] A long poem by Schubert on the subject of God's omnipotence is mentioned by his friend Anton Holzapfel. Unfortunately, the poem has been lost.[7]

His friend Huttenbrenner recalled asking Schubert "whether he did not also want to try setting prose to music and chose, for this purpose, the text from St. John, Chapter VI, verse 58: 'This is that bread which came down from heaven: not as your fathers did eat manna and are dead: he that eats of this bread shall live for ever.' He solved this problem wonderfully in twenty-four bars, which I still possess as a very precious souvenir of him. He chose for it the solemn key of E major and set the above verse for a soprano voice, with figured bass accompaniment."[8]

Schubert referred to his faith in his letters, thanking God for his talents.[9] In 1825, he wrote home describing the way his audience responded to a new sacred work he had composed. It "grips every soul and turns it to devotion," he wrote. Concerning his audience, he remarked that they "wondered greatly at my piety."[10] He concluded, "I think this is due to the fact that I have never forced devotion in myself and never compose hymns or prayers of that kind unless it overcomes me unawares; but then it is usually the right and true devotion."[11]

Other letters reveal different sides of his character. In one he humorously solicits funds from his brother with the biblical quote, "Let him that hath two coats give one to the poor."[12] In another, he deplores certain music that "engenders in people not love but madness: which rouses them to scornful laughter instead of lifting up their thoughts to God."[13] In still another, he explodes with revulsion at the sight of a cross and a chapel that were raised to observe the site of a bloody battle. "These sacred symbols are intended partly to commemorate and partly to expiate a horrible crime. Oh, dear Christ, over how many deeds of shame must Thou lend Thy countenance? Of Him who in Himself is the most convincing testimony to our human wickedness, they erect an image everywhere in wood and stone, as much as to say, 'See here, we have trampled under our profane feet the most perfect creation of the great God. What shall hinder us then in annihilating easily the rest of ordinary mankind?'"[14]

In 1816 Schubert began to keep a diary, noting odd thoughts that occurred to him in solitude: "Man comes into the world with faith, which is far superior to knowledge and understanding, for in order to understand a thing one must first of all believe in it. Reason is nothing more than analyzed belief."[15] Mired in poverty, he once wrote, "A man endures misfortune without complaint, but he feels it the more acutely. Why does God endow us with compassion?" Another time he wrote, "The world resembles a stage on which every man is playing a part. Approval or blame will follow in the world to come."[16] His day-to-day difficulties may have turned Schubert's longings toward God. "It sometimes seems to me as if I did not belong to this world at all," he observed.[17]

But it is Schubert's music itself that reveals the composer's faith most clearly. His biographer Peggy Woodford notes that, despite our lack of many details concerning Schubert's life and beliefs, all of his music presupposes "an intense spiritual life."[18] His songs in particular, she writes, "imply that he was a deeply religious man."[19]

Musicologist Carl A. Abram, writing about the last of Schubert's great masses, states, "Certainly it is impossible to doubt the heartfelt piety and God-fearing humility which shines through even the most extended and turbulent of all the Masses, namely, the E-flat major. Only a truly religious spirit could prompt Schubert to have the chorus cry out utterly alone, as though from the wilderness of despair, at the beginning of the *Gloria*. Only an inner longing for divine help and release could have sustained the brooding and melancholy Schubert of the last years (the Mass was composed in the last six months before his death) in the long, imploring sob, *eleison*, which occurs shortly before the end of the *Kyrie*. . . . this Mass is undeniably an expression of strong religious devotion."[20] The composition moved Oskar Bie to write, "It is the song of Christ's incarnation. The whole choir bears the crucifixion."[21]

Victory over death is a main theme in all the Schubert *Novalis* settings, according to renowned baritone Dietrich Fischer-Dieskau. In a study of Schubert songs, he wrote, "Schubert's struggle with this phenomenon is manifested here as the personal experience of an act of faith."[22] Schubert wrote a considerable amount of sacred music, notable for its diversity. Among these works are his *Hymn to Faith, Hope and Charity*,[23] the sacred cantata *Miriam's Song of Victory*,[24] and the *Hymn to the Holy Spirit*, over which the composer appears to have taken great pains.[25] Furthermore, Schubert left behind an unfinished Easter cantata based on the biblical account of Jesus raising Lazarus from the dead.[26]

Schubert was raised Catholic, yet he wrote music for other churches, especially in his later years.[27] He even omitted the words, *Credo in unam sanctam catholicam it apostolicam ecclesiam* ("I believe in one holy Catholic and apostolic church") from his masses.[28] For years, he longed for a Kapellmeister post where he might work for a local church,[29] but such an offer never materialized.

Perhaps because he was never confined by a job to a specific church, his spiritual life was as individualistic and personal as his musical gifts were unique and self-taught. Through the tribulations of his tragic life, it was the combination of two elements in his nature—his faith in God and his God-given talent—that enabled him to create without applause or acclaim the many masterpieces we treasure today.

Some Thoughts on Schubert: Sincerity

Listening to Schubert's music, especially the hundreds of beautiful songs that flowed from his pen, the simple sincerity of the composer's soul is evident. His music is transparent and is seldom mistaken for works of any other composer. He refused to look upon his talent as a tool for making money. Rather, he poured out his heart into every work.

Dietrich Fischer-Dieskau, famed for singing Schubert lieder, has said, "No matter how great our admiration for Schubert may be, we [those who perform his songs] only realize later in life what it is that raises him far above the level of other composers: Schubert is *authentic*." Schubert never effected false pretenses, either in his music or in his life. No wonder he made many friends. Those around him believed they really knew the whole man, without reservation, and they were right. In the stuffy, ostentatious society of Vienna, such openness and simplicity must have been a breath of fresh air.

In retrospect, Schubert clearly made mistakes in his life that inevitably resulted in devastating consequences. Yet in his principal calling, to be an original and innovative composer, he refused to compromise. Doubtless he could have achieved greater financial success writing trite nonsense for the multitudes. For Schubert, this would have been flagrant duplicity.

The immediate price for this sincerity was far greater than the absence of universal fame: It resulted in a life of impoverishment. But the fruit of this sacrifice is still being appreciated by generations who have loved the beauty and simplicity of Schubert's many works. Had this composer been anything less than sincere, he might have opted to seize immediate gratification. Instead, he chose the way of integrity, and we reap the rewards of his legacy.

Recommended Listening

Orchestral Music: 9 symphonies, notably *Symphony no. 8 in B Minor* ("Unfinished"); *Symphony no. 9 in C Major* ("The Great")

Chamber Music: *Quartet in A Minor*; *Quartet in D Minor* ("Death and the Maiden"); *Quintet in C Major* for strings; *Quintet in A Major* for piano and strings ("Die Forelle")

Piano Music: *Moments Musicaux*; impromptus; *Sonata in C Minor*

Vocal Music: More than 600 songs, including *Erlkonig*, *Die Forelle*, *Tod und das Madchen*, *Ave Maria*, *An die Musik*, *Gretchen am Spinnrade*, *Heidenroslein*

"Pray to God that He may create in us a clean heart and renew a right spirit within us."

Felix

MENDELSSOHN

1809–1847

The visitor arrives late, tapping at the door almost impercep-
tibly in case the family is asleep. When no one answers, he lets
himself in and makes his way toward his friend's music study. He
knows it well from engaging in many friendly dialogues there that
have continued long into the night.

As he enters, he sees his friend engrossed in his Bible. The
visitor stands quietly, awkwardly, for a moment. Finally, the mas-
ter of the house glances up at the visitor, showing no sign of sur-
prise and offering no greeting. "Listen," he says, and excitedly
begins to read aloud: "And behold, the Lord passed by. . . ." He
reads on and on, his voice rising in pitch as the drama of the pas-
sage overwhelms him.

The visitor recognizes the story of Elijah, when suddenly the
reading stops. "Would not that be splendid for an oratorio?" asks
Felix Mendelssohn, setting the Bible on his desk and searching his
friend's face for a reaction. Thus the greatest oratorio of the nine-
teenth century was conceived.

Many of the great composers seem to have suffered more than
their share of life's misfortune and frustration. In sharp
contrast, Felix Mendelssohn led, for the most part, a happy and
successful life. Born into a wealthy and cultured family, his

remarkable talents were encouraged from the start, and he brilliantly pursued an abundance of musical endeavors.

Rather than producing a spoiled cavalier, his cultivated upbringing gave Mendelssohn a sensitive and charitable spirit. In a typically benevolent frame of mind, he wrote a friend, "I dislike nothing more than finding fault with a man's nature or talent; it only depresses and worries and does no good; one cannot add a cubit to one's stature, all striving and struggling are useless there, so one has to be silent about it, and let the responsibility rest with God."[1]

His grandfather, Moses Mendelssohn, had been an important Jewish philosopher, yet the composer's father, Abraham, was somewhat uncertain in his beliefs.[2] At first, he raised his children "without religion in any form,"[3] though his brother-in-law was strongly influencing him toward Christianity.[4] In those times Jews encountered deep prejudice throughout Europe. Only with the greatest difficulty had the Mendelssohn family acquired a degree of wealth.

Once when he was a child, Mendelssohn ran home in tears from chorus practice. The chorus had been singing a passage from Bach's *St. Matthew Passion* when another youth hissed mockingly, "The Jew-boy raises his voice to Christ!" Seeing his children tormented because of their religious heritage was too much for Abraham; a desire for his children's happiness rather than personal spiritual conviction finally persuaded him to have them baptized and raised in the Christian faith.[5]

Yet Mendelssohn, far from resenting his forced entry into the new faith, embraced it fervently his entire life.[6] In his manuscripts this young prodigy often penned a prayerful exclamation: *Lass es gelingen Gott!* ("Let it succeed, God!") or *Hilf Du mit* ("Help along").[7] His biographer, Eric Werner, writes, "He was faithful to the Christian religion and took it seriously.[8] "Reverence, fear of God, the sense of praise, of gratitude, of bitter complaints and of pride in one's faith, all these lay in his personality. He had great respect for the Biblical Word."[9]

When he matured, Mendelssohn joined the Lutheran church, although he attended worship services of various denominations.

At one point, he inclined toward Catholicism, but his passionate love for the music of the Protestant Bach anchored him to Lutheranism.[10]

One of Mendelssohn's many illustrious accomplishments was to "rediscover" and champion Bach's music, which had become neglected and all but forgotten. He considered Bach's work "the greatest Christian music in the world."[11] In fact, he held one particular Bach chorus in such high regard that he wrote, "If life had taken hope and faith from me, this single chorus would restore all."[12] From the time he was a boy badgered for his Jewish roots, he was spellbound by the *St. Matthew Passion*. He and a friend from the theater mounted it in a full performance, after decades of obscurity. When Mendelssohn mounted the podium to conduct, he found that a different musical score had been mistakenly placed in front of him. He conducted the entire composition from memory, even turning the pages of the incorrect score, so as not to alarm the unknowing soloists. His devotion to the Baroque master initiated the grand "Bach revival" of the nineteenth century.

Mendelssohn excelled as a composer, a pianist, a conductor, and the founder of the Leipzig Conservatory of Music. Not that his life was always idyllic; he experienced a number of personality conflicts as a conductor and administrator. But his talent won consistent acclaim, and his acquaintances included the finest musical geniuses of Europe: Schumann, Liszt, Wagner, Paganini, Weber, and Chopin, to name a few.

Mendelssohn never hesitated to display his faith openly to those around him. Fellow composer Berlioz, a radical freethinker, once recalled, "Mendelssohn believed firmly in his Lutheran religion and I sometimes shocked him profoundly by laughing at the Bible."[13] Another fellow composer later recorded his admiration of Mendelssohn: "So richly favored and endowed, so beloved and admired, and at the same time so strong in mind and character, that he never once let slip the bridle of religious discipline, nor the just sense of modesty and humility, nor ever fell short of his standard of duty."[14] His wife, Cecile, the daughter of a well-known clergyman of the French Reformed Church,[15] was a pious believer and a woman of prayer.[16]

For Mendelssohn, the Bible served as the cornerstone of daily life as well as the inspiration for much of his work. When he set passages of Scripture to music, he was painstakingly precise about the wording.[17] According to a friend who knew him well, "He felt that all faith must be based on Holy Writ."[18] Mendelssohn congratulated his librettist, noting "I am glad to learn that you are searching out the always heart-affecting sense of the scriptural words."[19] When the biblical text was altered, Mendelssohn observed, "I have time after time had to restore the precise text of the Bible. It is the best in the end."[20]

Mendelssohn's letters reveal a profound faith in God.[21] Echoing the words of a psalm, he wrote, "Pray to God that He may create in us a clean heart and renew a right spirit within us."[22] To his nephew, he wrote, "Nothing is attained, without the fulfillment of one fervent wish—May God be with you! This prayer comprises consolation and strength, and also cheerfulness in days to come."[23]

His own work as a composer blended his belief in divine inspiration with his Protestant work ethic. "I know perfectly well that no musician can make his thoughts or his talents different to what Heaven has made them; but I also know that if Heaven had given him good ones, he must also be able to develop them properly."[24] He composed a great deal of sacred music, notably his celebrated oratorios *Elijah* and *Saint Paul*. The story of Paul's dramatic conversion to Christianity touched Mendelssohn deeply. As he composed it, he wrote, "I must not make any mistakes."[25] His letters speak of a holy zeal to complete the project,[26] and in the process he devoured everything he could read on Greek and church history, as well as daily life in the time Paul lived.[27]

Mendelssohn's music is universal in its appeal, and his compositions run the gamut from "Ave Maria" to texts of Martin Luther set to music.[28] He felt dissatisfied with music created by many Catholic composers, observing, "I have found, to my astonishment, that the Catholics, who have had music in their churches for several centuries, and sing a musical Mass every Sunday if possible, in their principal churches, do not to this day possess one which can be considered even tolerably good, or in fact which is not actually distasteful and operatic.... Were I a Catholic, I would set to work at a Mass this very evening; and, whatever it might turn out, it would at all events be the only Mass written with a constant remembrance of its sacred purpose."[29]

Mendelssohn demonstrated a careful authenticity in composing sacred music, and the same trait is evident in his personal views on how the Christian faith should be interpreted and lived. Once, he found himself the object of praise by members of the "heavenly minded" Pietist movement. He responded, "So I am said to be a saint! If this is intended to convey what I conceive to be the meaning of the word, and what your expressions lead me to think you also understand by it, then I can only say that, alas! I am not so, though every day of my life I strive with greater earnestness, according to my ability, more and more to resemble this character. I know indeed that I can never hope to be altogether a saint, but if I ever approach to one, it will be well.

"If people, however, understand by the word 'saint' a Pietist, one of those who lay their hands on their laps and expect that Providence will do their work for them, and who, instead of striving in their vocation to press on towards perfection, talk of a heavenly calling being incompatible with an earthly one, and are incapable of loving with their whole hearts any human being, or anything on earth, then God be praised! Such a one I am not, and hope never to become, so long as I live. And though I am sincerely desirous to live piously, and really to be so, I hope this does not necessarily entail the other character."[30]

Mendelssohn's life was cut short after he received the crushing news that his sister and close companion had suddenly died. He lost consciousness and fell, rupturing a blood vessel in his head. He never recovered, remaining very ill until his death a few months later at the age of thirty-eight. Even when he knew death was approaching, he cheerfully and steadfastly maintained his faith. Mendelssohn wrote, "A great chapter is now ended, and neither the title nor even the first word of the next is yet written. But

God will make it all right one day; this suits the beginning and the end of all chapters."[31]

Some Thoughts on Mendelssohn: Optimism

Mendelssohn's life was particularly happy and successful, especially in comparison with so many other composers. Furthermore, Mendelssohn maintained a very positive attitude toward life, full of optimism, confidence, and expectation for the future. The question then arises: Did his good attitude develop in response to all the splendid circumstances in his life, or did the splendid circumstances arise because of his optimistic attitude?

Whatever the outcome of such a debate, one thing is clear: Mendelssohn's positive outlook was an invaluable asset. He expected excellent results and he generally got them, even in some very large-scale musical ventures. He expected to be a world-class musician, and he became one even in his teens. He expected the world to react enthusiastically to his "rediscovery" of Bach's music—and it did and still is! He expected to get a principal conducting post, and in his mid twenties he was given Leipzig's prestigious Gewandhaus Orchestra. He expected to create a great music school, and in 1843 founded the renowned Leipzig Conservatory of Music. He even expected to have a passionate, loving marriage with Cecile, and he did; historical accounts indicate their "love story" could have provided the script for a romantic novel.

Of course, none of these accomplishments came without effort. Mendelssohn's own teacher remained skeptical about the first Bach performance. Before he gained the Gewandhaus position, Mendelssohn had to endure the frustration of directing a miserable musical season at Dusseldorf. And before the Conservatory could take shape, he struggled to obtain not only the permission but the financial backing of an indifferent king.

Yet it seems Mendelssohn never gave a thought to the possibility of failure. He knew what he wanted to do, and he resolved to see it done. His name was quite appropriate: "Felix" in Latin means "happy man." He lived his life as though he considered this name a prophetic gift. Not that he dealt in bravado or exulted in applause; his quiet confidence gave him an unassuming and modest temperament. He simply expected to be successful, and his accomplishments in thirty-eight years offer convincing proof of the benefits of his optimism.

Recommended Listening

Orchestral music: 5 symphonies, notably no. 4 ("Italian") and no. 5 ("Reformation"); *Concerto in E Minor* for violin and orchestra; *A Midsummer Night's Dream*, suite; *Fingal's Cave* ("Hebrides") *Overture*

Chamber music: *Octet in E-flat Major*

Piano music: *Songs Without Words*

Oratorio: *Elijah; St. Paul*

Choral music: *Psalms; Hymns of Praise*

"Oh, how good God is!"

Frédéric
CHOPIN

1810–1849

The household was cheerless, as the last bags were packed for the journey. The three young girls were fighting back tears, while the father comforted his wife, who was openly weeping. The day was November 2, 1830, and the only son of that family was setting out from his native Warsaw to make his fortune in the world.

The young man felt a mixture of excitement for the promise of a great future and sadness to leave those whom he loved so deeply. As his eyes looked for the last time on the rooms he had known since infancy, he saw the piano on which he had spent so many hours. And now the last warm embraces of his sisters and parents. His mother whispered to him, "Frédéric, thou wilt be a great musician. Thy Poland will be proud of thee."

Soon the carriage was away, and the young man tearfully watched as his home shrank from sight. Misgivings came to his mind. Could he do it? Would he be appreciated in the great cities of Vienna and Paris as he was in his own country? Doubt and uncertainty flooded his soul.

But at the coach's first stop, he had a heartening surprise, which had been prepared by his music teacher, Joseph Elsner. The young man was startled to see a small choir assembled, singing a cantata written by Elsner as a farewell present. They sang:

"Born among Polish fields,
May your talent bring you fame wherever you go.

Although you leave your native land,
Still will your heart remain with us!"
The young man bounded from his coach for a score of hearty
handshakes. Finally, the time for departure arrived. His teacher
presented a silver urn filled with the soul of Poland, which the
youth would carry throughout his travels. Elsner smiled through
his tears as embraced his greatest student, Frédéric Chopin, who
was on his way to enthrall all of Europe with his music.

Chopin is unique among the great masters in that his compositions are almost exclusively for one instrument, the solo
piano. Even in his other works, the few songs and chamber music,
as well as his two concerti for piano, the keyboard is always uti-
lized. No other composer in history has made such a rich contri-
bution to piano literature.

Like his romantic music, the life of Chopin was filled with
emotional joys and sorrows. From a spiritual point of view, it was a
three-stage journey: He was raised within a loving, religious family,
then drifted away from his faith while making his career in Paris,
and finally returned to God soon before his untimely death at the
age of thirty-nine.

In his youth, Chopin had the two greatest benefits a talented
musician can be given: wonderful supportive parents and a brilliant encouraging teacher. He was the only boy in a family of four
children, all of whom were attracted to music. The household was
harmonious, and his parents were delighted with their son's con-
spicuous talent.

Although the Chopin family was far from wealthy (his father
was a French teacher in various schools), they happily sacrificed
to find Frédéric adequate music teachers. They somehow arranged
to buy a grand piano, even though a spinet or clavichord might
have better fit their Warsaw apartment. His first instructor introduced him to Bach and Mozart, and by his ninth year he had suc-
cessfully performed for a local prince and Tzar Alexander I, who
rewarded him with a diamond ring.

The boy progressed so rapidly that it was soon obvious that a more expert teacher was necessary. When Chopin met Joseph Elsner, the director of the Warsaw Conservatory, he found exactly what was needed. This teacher had the wonderful ability to bring out the very best in his students. He insisted, "It is not enough for a student to equal or surpass his master; he should create an individuality of his own." Realizing Chopin's extraordinary talent, Elsner did everything possible to nurture it.

Like Beethoven several decades earlier, Chopin visited Vienna, the musical capital of Europe in 1829. His debut was successful, and this taste of victory—coupled with a youthful craving to see the world—gave him the hope of becoming an international performer. Back in Warsaw, young Chopin was restless and bored. In 1830, he determined to seek his fortune abroad.

He traveled to Vienna, Munich, Stuttgart, and Paris, expecting to continue to London. But in the French capital, he was so embraced by the fashionable salons that he made Paris his new home. Suddenly the young pianist-composer from Poland was the talk of the town. As many as thirty different salons fought for his attention. He fraternized with the rich and powerful, with beautiful women and influential men.

Unfortunately, the moral level at this time in Paris—and especially in this social stratum—was notoriously low. This fact was so evident that even the official guidebook designed to attract tourists to France warned those visitors who did not feel strong enough to resist the temptations of this city to escape as soon as possible before they were engulfed by this "treacherous precipice of sin and debauchery."[1]

At this pivotal time of his life, far from the guidance of his parents, Chopin wandered from the faith of his childhood. Raised in a devout Catholic family, Frédéric had always been faithful to his church.[2] His mother was exceptionally pious,[3] and his letters throughout his life often refer to fond memories of childhood experiences at church.[4] His parents continued to pray for their distant son and wrote him reassuring letters: ""Your old father and mother live only for you and pray God every day to bless and keep you."

But in the salons of Paris, such memories were blurred by new and overwhelming influences. As his biographer James Huneker describes, "He had good friends, but many bad friends. These bad friends were his flatterers, that is, his enemies, men and women without principles, or rather with bad principles."[5] An indication of Chopin's fashionable colleagues is given in a conversation noted in his journal: "Who invented music?" asks Athman. I answer, "Musicians." He isn't satisfied, he insists. I answer gravely that God did. "No," he replies immediately, "it was the devil."[6]

In this period of disorientation and spiritual confusion, Chopin met the infamous French novelist who called herself George Sands. At first, his sensitive nature and traditional upbringing caused him to be repulsed by her unsavory reputation, as well as by her rebellious practices of smoking cigars and wearing men's clothing. "What a repellent woman she is," he protested. "Is she really a woman? I'm inclined to doubt it."

Yet she was intensely attracted to Chopin, and her authoritative and dynamic personality proved too much for him. Soon they were seen together everywhere. She invited him to spend the summer of 1838 with her at her country home, and for the next eight years they endured a stormy romance.

Even in this phase of spiritual drought, there are indications that Chopin's faith was trying to resurface. In her autobiography, George Sands' *Story of My Life*, some passages seem to indicate that Chopin's constant and unshaken faith deeply impressed her.[7] She complained that, "He was a prisoner of Catholic dogma," and she also stated that Chopin was "irrevocably attached to the church."[8]

He spoke to her of "the lovely faith of his childhood,"[9] and was profoundly shocked by her disrespect for traditional Christianity.[10]

For much of this period, Chopin was deeply distressed with inner turmoil. He felt, to use his own words, "like the thinnest string of the violin stretched on a double bass."[11] George Sands would some day reveal the reason for Chopin's internal anguish. She wrote, "Our relationship, although it gave him here on earth all the delights of Heaven, provoked in his soul a permanent fear of

Hell, since this relationship had not been blessed by the church."[12] In Alfred Cortot's excellent book, *In Search of Chopin*, he explains that the composer's feeling for religion "led him to fear the threat of punishment ascribed by the Church to all those who transgress the laws of chastity outside the bonds of holy matrimony."[13]

Surely some of Chopin's turmoil had to do with his sensitive conscience, living in a world where his deepest beliefs had so little encouragement. There is evidence that in this period of his life he kept his religious feelings to himself.[14] His fellow pianist Franz Liszt, who knew him very well, testified that Chopin was a man of prayer.[15] But Liszt also remarked, "Sincerely religious, and attached to Catholicity, Chopin never touched upon this subject, but held his faith without attracting attention to it. One might have been acquainted with him for a long time, without knowing exactly what his religious opinions were."[16]

An interesting picture of this "private" Chopin is given by one of his servants, Jan. Concerning his employer, he writes that, "He was religious but, as I could observe, he didn't like to let it be known to anybody. Not out of curiosity but for fear of an accident (because I often saw him in a state close to fainting), I watched by night, through the keyhole in order to see how my master was getting on. And I saw him on his knees, leaning on his bed. He remained a long time in this position and prayed eagerly.[17]

Chopin scholar Matteo Glinski, summarizing this difficult time in the composer's life says, "An avalanche of new experiences eclipsed his memories of the atmosphere of his paternal home but, with maturity, his religious feeling once again became intense. We find God and Divine Providence mentioned more and more often in Chopin's letters. Chopin revealed to one of his beloved friends that he prayed for him and that he knew the Holy Scripture by heart. Liszt informs us that from the first years of his sojourn in Paris, Chopin was always very closely attached to a Polish priest who was probably his confessor."[18]

The tension Chopin felt at this time of his life was finally resolved in a painful break with George Sands. One might think that with this lurid relationship behind him, years of inspirational work would now open up before him. But it was not to be. His health, which had never been robust, was now broken. His body was rapidly giving way to consumption, which the medical practices of his day could do little to cure.

In 1848 he took one last trip to England and Scotland. From this journey there is a letter that again shows spiritual concern. The ever-Catholic Chopin writes of a, "Mrs. Erskine, who is a very religious Protestant, good soul, would perhaps like to make a Protestant of me: she brings me the Bible, talks about the soul, quotes the psalms to me; she is religious, poor thing, but she is greatly concerned about my soul. She is always telling me that the other world is better than this one; and I know all by heart, and answer with quotations from Scripture and explain that I understand and know about it."[19]

But his health continued to deteriorate. By the time he returned to Paris he was dying. Yet it is at this very late time in his life that his faith would blossom to its fullest. The many different accounts of Chopin's last days are sometimes difficult to reconcile, but all agree that the composer made a dramatic return to his Christian faith.

This conversion was precipitated by the prayers of those who knew and loved him. For years, his parents had offered their prayers on his behalf, and now others would join in this effort. His friends Princesses Sapieha, Norwid, and Zaleski talked to him about the next life, and Chopin would ask them to pray for him and listened with devotion when they once or twice did so at his bedside.[20]

As Chopin's condition became critical, the Abbe Jelowicki, who had known the composer for many years, was sent for. Aware of the life that Chopin had known in the salons of Paris, the Abbe was at first concerned that his old friend would show little interest in his faith. "Yet I clung to the conviction that the grace of God would obtain the victory over this rebellious soul, even if I knew not how. After all my exertions, prayer remained my only refuge."[21]

After spending much time with Chopin, the composer told the Abbe that he had not confessed for many years, but that he would do so now. When the confession was over and the last word of the absolution spoken, Chopin embraced his confessor with both arms and exclaimed: "Thanks! Thanks!"[22]

The Abbe Jelowicki later remembered, "Then I experienced an inexpressible joy mixed with an indescribable anguish. How should I receive this precious soul so as to give it to God? I fell on my knees, and cried to God with all the energy of my faith: 'You alone receive it, O my God!' And I held out to Chopin the image of the crucified Savior, pressing it firmly in his two hands without saying a word. Then fell from his eyes big tears. 'Do you believe?' I asked him.

'I believe.'

'Do you believe as your mother taught you?'

'As my mother taught me.' And, his eyes fixed on the image of his Savior, he confessed while shedding torrents of tears."[23]

The Abbe also wrote, "From this hour he was a saint. The death struggle began and lasted four days. Patience, trust in God, even joyful confidence, never left him in spite of all his sufferings, till the last breath. He was really happy, and called himself happy. In the midst of the sharpest sufferings he expressed only ecstatic joy, touching love of God, thankfulness that I had led him back to God, contempt of the world and its goods, and a wish for a speedy death. He blessed his friends, and when, after an apparently last crisis, he saw himself surrounded by the crowd that day and night filled his chamber, he asked me, 'Why do they not pray?' At these words all fell on their knees, and even the Protestants joined in the litanies and prayers for the dying. Day and night he held my hand, and would not let me leave him. 'No, you will not leave me at the last moment,' he said, and leaned on my breast as a little child in a moment of danger hides itself in its mother's breast."[24]

In his recorded comments to those present it becomes clear that a spiritual change had come upon Chopin. When a doctor sought to console him, the composer remarked, "God shows man a rare favour when He reveals to him the moment of the approach of death; this grace He shows me. Do not disturb me."[25] He later said to the physicians, "Let me die. Do not keep me longer in this world of exile. Let me die; why do you prolong my life when I have renounced all things and God has enlightened my soul? God calls me; why do you keep me back?"[26]

Another time he said, "O lovely science, that only lets one suffer longer! Could it give me back my strength, qualify me to do any good, to make any sacrifice—but a life of fainting, of grief, of pain to all who love me, to prolong such a life—O lovely science!" Then he said again: "You let me suffer cruelly. Perhaps you have erred about my sickness. But God errs not. He punishes me, and I bless him therefore. Oh, how good is God to punish me here below! Oh, how good God is!"[27]

His friend and fellow composer Liszt wrote that Chopin "thought of death with Christian calm and resignation."[28] Several of his last comments are especially poignant. "I love God and man," he said. "I am happy so to die; do not weep, my sister. My friends, do not weep. I am happy. I feel that I am dying. Farewell, pray for me!"[29]

Chopin died at about two o'clock in the morning of October 17, 1849. The cause of his death was given as tuberculosis of the lungs and larynx.[30] He was buried with the Polish soil that his music teacher had given him on the day he left his beloved country. Before he died, Chopin expressed the wish that Mozart's *Requiem* be sung at his funeral.[31]

Some Thoughts on Chopin: Repentance

Many people, as they contemplate the tragically short life of Frédéric Chopin, think only of the music that would never be written. But as we consider his profound conversion before his death, we are aware of spiritual aspects that are often forgotten. Suppose Chopin had lived a long life like Stravinsky—who did not become a Christian until well into his forties, and then wrote a great deal of music to the glory of God. Who knows but that Chopin could have followed his rebirth with a life that might have had a significant spiritual impact on the world.

When one reads about Chopin's final days, certainly the composer's heartfelt repentance is apparent to all. Yet even before his pivotal encounter with God, there are signs of a troubled conscience seeking to atone for his sins. As George Sands recalled that their relationship "provoked in his soul a permanent fear of Hell," one can imagine a sense of relief he must have felt to have that association finally end. His joyous comments on his deathbed about God's chastisement confirms a penitent soul: "But God errs not. He punishes me, and I bless him therefore. Oh, how good is God to punish me here below! Oh, how good God is!"

Another illustration of Chopin's heart of repentance concerns his supreme gratitude toward the man who had led him back to the Lord. Before he died, he directed that the ministry receive twenty times the sum that was usually given to perform last rites. When the Abbe forcefully protested that this amount was far too much, Chopin rejoined, "No, no, this is not too much, for what I have received is priceless."

The last days of Chopin give us a model for every day of our own lives. Throughout the intense physical pain, he portrayed a man who was truly contrite as well as joyful that he had been forgiven. The Abbe Jelowicki recalls, "His patience and resignation to the will of God did not abandon him up to the last minute." Chopin smiled at his old friend and murmured, "Without you I should have crocked like a pig." He took a cross and placed it on his heart, confessing his thankfulness: "Now I am at the source of Blessedness."

Recommended Listening

Orchestral Music: 2 concerti for piano and orchestra
Chamber Music: *Piano Trio; Sonata for Cello and Piano*
Piano Music: 24 etudes, 26 preludes, 11 polonaises, 19 nocturnes, 54 mazurkas, 3 sonatas, and many other smaller pieces

"Through Christ alone, through resigned suffering in God, salvation and rescue come to us."

Franz
LISZT

1811–1886

*The music emanating from the piano fills the room with
exquisite sound. A hushed audience sits spellbound, as if they
were in the presence of a seasoned master musician. Yet before
their eyes is a twelve-year-old boy, his legs stretching to reach the
pedals beneath the piano and his smooth face furrowed in close
concentration.*

*He appears almost at one with the instrument he plays, strik-
ing the keys with a remarkable combination of authority and sensitivity. Not since Mozart have the concertgoers of Vienna seen such
a prodigy. They exchange hurried glances of approval and disbelief.*

*When the music stops, the audience thunders its applause. A
man awkwardly steps toward the piano as a whisper makes its
way throughout the hall: The great Beethoven is here. Even
though he is almost completely deaf, Beethoven recognizes the rare
talent before him. He sweeps the boy up in his arms and kisses
him on the cheek. For the rest of his life, the moment remains
seared in the memory of the boy, Franz Liszt. Within months,
Liszt would be proclaimed by the public to be the "eighth wonder
of the world."*

The Age of Romanticism produced many contradictions in art,
politics, and religion. It was a time of emerging self-expression
and individualism and a time of breaking new ground, expanding

musical horizons. Innovation marked the Romantics and so did sentimentality. Few individuals personified these incongruities more completely than the pianist-composer Franz Liszt. His imaginative career generated a host of legendary events. Scholars are still at odds over the authenticity of such incidents as that described above, even though it was described by Liszt himself. His many-sided personality defies easy analysis, and it is particularly difficult to reconcile his devout spirituality with his outrageous lifestyle.

On one hand, Liszt was a fervent Christian all his life and even entered the priesthood when he was in his fifties. On the other hand, he was an incorrigible womanizer who careered from one glamorous affair to another, often with women who appeared to share his sincere religious outlook on life. Above all, he was a master musician—possibly the greatest virtuoso of his century—who from boyhood dazzled the adoring audiences of Europe. These internal inconsistencies wrestled within him throughout his long and colorful life.

"From youth up, Franz's spirit was naturally inclined to devotion, and his passionate feeling for art was blended with a piety which was characterized by all the frankness of his age," reads an entry in the diary of his father, who died when Liszt was sixteen.[1] As a child, Liszt's favorite reading materials included the Bible, St. Thomas à Kempis's *Imitation of Christ*, and the lives of the saints. Hungering for stories about the lives of the apostles, he begged his mother to read from the Bible. The narrative of Christ's Passion moved him to tears, and the simple ceremony of bedtime prayer brought him great comfort and joy.[2]

Liszt's consuming interest in Christianity made him long to enter the priesthood, and he frequently implored his parents to enroll him in seminary.[3] His parents, both devout Catholics, instead chose to encourage his musical career. Once when Liszt persisted in talking about becoming a priest, his father brought him up short: "You belong to music, not to religion. Love God, be good and honest, and you will reach the highest summits in art, a vocation for which the natural gifts Providence has bestowed upon you have destined you."[4]

Undeterred, Liszt's passion for God intensified. At age seventeen, he pleaded tearfully, once again, to be allowed to enter the Paris Seminary: "I hoped it might be granted to me to live the life of the saints and perhaps die the death of the martyrs."[5] Even his mother, who gave him a strong sense of religion and duty,[6] was troubled by the raw emotion of his letters. He later wrote to her, "You know, dearest mother, how during the years of my youth, I dreamed myself incessantly into the world of the saints. Nothing seemed to me so self-evident as heaven, nothing so true and so rich in blessedness as the goodness and compassion of God."[7]

Yet despite all his religious fervor, Liszt led a life of epic sensual self-indulgence. Throughout most of his adult life, Liszt participated in a series of celebrated love affairs. He became intimate with well-known and highly placed women such as the Countess Marie d'Agoult and the Princess Carolyne Sayn-Wittgenstein, a wealthy patron remembered for her mystical religiosity and her incessant cigar smoking![8]

Much has been written already about this composer's long romances, with so little emphasis on his faith. And it is true that Liszt never married, even after living for years with one lover or another and fathering several illegitimate children. Liszt showed no outward sign of embarrassment or guilt over his affairs, and he appeared rather indifferent to the opinions and the censure of others.[9] Yet living in a state of blatant contradiction between belief and action could not be completely dismissed. He appeared painfully aware of the inconsistencies of his life, however, which caused persistent inner turmoil and periods of depression.[10]

Thwarted in his youthful ambition to become a priest, Liszt found in music an outlet to express his faith as well as his extraordinary talent. His renown as a virtuoso pianist made him the most sought-after musician in Europe. As a performer, a composer, and a teacher, he profoundly influenced other musicians of his day. Yet Liszt also believed he had a calling to compose church music. Writing to a friend in 1856, he claimed, "I have taken a serious stand as a religious, Catholic composer. Among the composers I know, none has a more intense and deeper feeling for religious music than your humble servant."[11]

Liszt pondered the future of church music, writing in an article, "The church composer is also preacher and priest and where words cannot suffice to convey the feeling, music gives them wings and transfigures them."[12] Biographer Eleanor Perenzi observes, "Liszt was probably the nineteenth century's greatest composer of religious music, alone in his blend of scholarship, originality and devotion."[13] Another biographer, van Wessem, wrote, "Liszt has never done anything without profound religious thought."[14]

As early as 1834, the composer himself insisted that music's purpose was, "to ennoble, to comfort, to purify man, to bless and praise God."[15] Liszt composed many works of sacred music, both in choral genre, such as his settings of five psalms, masses, and oratorios; and in such piano pieces as the *Harmonies poetiques et religieuses*, the two *Legendes* and the last book of the *Annees de pelerinage*.

A particular depth of inspiration appears evident in his spiritual compositions. Concerning his *Solemn Mass*, he wrote Wagner that he had "prayed this Mass rather than composed."[16] Liszt composed his *XIIIth Psalm* "weeping blood," as he subsequently wrote.[17] In his last decades he was intrigued with the influence of the Gregorian chorale, as seen in such works as his *Via Crucis*.[18] For his greatest religious work, the massive oratorio *Christus*, Liszt wrote his own Latin libretto composed of extracts from the Holy Scriptures.[19]

The religion of this romantic was not a thoughtless, superstitious trust in a "Genie-God" but a firm faith in the deity who created the universe and remains active in it. Concerning this balance between stark rationalism and unpredictable mysticism, he writes that he "knew neither ecstasy nor visions."[20] He makes it clear that his beliefs are firmly rooted in conventional Christianity: "The ardent longing for the Cross, and the elevation of the Cross have always been my true, my innermost vocation."[21]

One person who distinctly influenced the composer was the Abbe de Lamennais, a devout writer who attacked the excesses of the Catholic Church and became one of the most prominent ministers in Europe. Liszt spent hours in fellowship with this man who loved the arts and God. The Abbe once wrote, "God is the greatest artist, his work is the world."[22] Their admiration was mutual: Liszt called Lamennais "fatherly friend and instructor,"[23] and the Abbe wrote Liszt that he would "glory and be proud to be one day called your disciple."[24] The musicologist Hugh Reginald Hawais, who knew them both, claimed it was Lamennais "who, more than any other, saved Liszt from drifting into the prevailing whirlpool of atheism."[25]

Letters Liszt wrote contain many references to his faith as well as his concern for others. In a letter to the younger composer, Richard Wagner, who later became Liszt's son-in-law, he wrote, "I will pray to God that he may powerfully illumine your heart through His faith and His love. You may scoff at this feeling as bitterly as you like. I cannot fail to see and desire in it the only salvation. Through Christ alone, through resigned suffering in God, salvation and rescue come to us."[26]

To Princess Marie zu Sayn-Wittgenstein he wrote, "May God keep you and lavish His blessings upon you. I will yet add what is said in the Gospel for Whitsunday: 'Let not your heart be troubled, neither let it be afraid.' Jesus gave you His peace—not as the world gives it."[27] In another letter, he writes encouragingly, "Carry out, then, with devout confidence, the inspiration of your heart, and the Lord's blessing be upon all upright souls."[28] In still another, he comforts: "Even on the most troubled days, there is certain peace for those who have the single felicity to be Christians."[29] Like the grand finales of many of his compositions, Liszt's letters often ended with a flourish: "May God be with you and may we love each other through Him, in this life and for Eternity!"[30]

Perhaps Liszt found the inner reconciliation he needed when, on April 25, 1865, he entered the Third Order of St. Francis of Assisi in Rome and became Abbe Liszt. Later in life he confessed, "If it had not been for music I should have devoted myself entirely to the church and would have become a Franciscan; it was my most innermost wish which led me to join the church that I wished to serve."[31]

Liszt considered his ordination the most important event of his life,[32] and he made elaborate preparations for it. He withdrew for a few days to the monastery of the Lazzaristi, and in a journal, he recorded how he spent his days. He rose from bed at half-past six, meditated alone in his cell, drank coffee in his room, attended Mass at half-past eight and, on Sundays, High Mass at half-past nine. Then came solitary Scripture readings, visits to the Holy Sacrament, and dinner in the refectory at midday, where he ate alone at a little table, unfortunately too far away from the pulpit to hear the readings given by a monk. In the afternoon, he walked in the garden, read the Bible, and spent one hour in solitary meditation. Supper was served at eight o'clock in silence, and religious discussions with the Superior followed until half-past nine. Lights-out occurred at ten o'clock.[33]

After a glamorous career as the world's greatest pianist, Liszt plunged into a life of startling austerity. At times, his experience in the priesthood must have seemed humiliating. After only ten days as an Abbe, Liszt had to practice his genuflections for almost three hours at the command of a religious superior.[34] But far and wide, people still appreciated Liszt. Even the pope himself admired and loved Liszt, calling him "his dear son" and "his Palestrina." The pope even told him that the law "ought to employ your music, in order to lead hardened criminals to repentance. Not one could resist, I am sure."[35]

Nevertheless, Liszt's life did not end in Rome. After a few years of seclusion, he began to travel, teach piano students, and occasionally even perform. All the proceeds of his concerts went to charity, not personal gain. As late as 1874, he turned down an offer for an American concert tour that would have guaranteed him 600,000 francs. Liszt remained an enigma to his last day, flirting with his students while in his seventies, yet maintaining throughout his life that he was "a true believer."[36]

Every six months, Liszt "consecrated a week to the salvation of his soul," one friend recalled.[37] Once on Good Friday, he spent the whole afternoon and the following day in church. On his knees before the image of Christ, Liszt cried unreservedly and smote his breast.[38] Two days later, on Easter Sunday, Liszt was over-heard speaking to a woman with whom he had been romantically associated. Perhaps he summed up the spiritual and emotional struggles he endured when he told her: "You see, my dear, there's nothing like putting your conscience in order."[39]

Some Thoughts on Liszt: Generosity

Accounts of the lives of great artists frequently dwell at length on details of their shortcomings. Portraying an artist's personal fail-ings is easier—and more popular—than appraising the nobler virtues that may invite emulation. Certainly the composer Liszt had his share of imperfections, especially in the extramarital cate-gory, which cannot be excused. Yet biographers consistently note that as a man, he was never hated. Rather he was respected, loved, and admired—and not merely for his talent. There was sound rea-son for this: Liszt possessed some exemplary personal virtues that should not be overlooked.

Ultimately, Liszt was a great philanthropist, giving liberally of his funds and his service to those in need. As a young man, his earnings went to pay his father's debts and to support his mother. At the height of his career, with potential millions right at his fin-gertips, he renounced giving concerts for money. Once he raised huge sums in Russia, for example, and then gave every cent to char-ity. His concerts also raised a small fortune for a "pension for desti-tute musicians." Hearing that a Beethoven Memorial was being planned, he immediately volunteered to help and paid for most of it himself. He had sacrificed so many of his worldly goods by 1865 that when he entered the Order of St. Francis, he possessed noth-ing but "his cassock, a little linen, and seven handkerchiefs."

Liszt was altruistic in other ways as well. Throughout his life he supported the music and careers of many other composers, often at his own expense. When he was appointed to the influen-tial position of Kapellmeister in Weimar, he unselfishly pro-grammed concert after concert championing the music of other composers rather than his own. Once, when Liszt heard that very few tickets were bought for an upcoming concert of Wagner's music, he volunteered to perform a Beethoven concerto on the program. The result was an immediate sellout.

Dozens of Liszt's piano pieces are actually his transcriptions of the works of others. This gave other musicians a greater opportunity to present their music to the public, which was a crucial need in the days before recorded music. And Liszt supported many composers financially, giving and loaning liberally, often without expecting to be repaid—particularly in the case of Wagner.

As the private teacher of a generation of pianists, Liszt refused to be paid for his invaluable lessons. The immense amount of time freely invested into his pupils would later yield an abundant musical harvest through such men as Von Bulow, Weingartner, Albenez, Bizet, Moszkowski, Joachim, Rosenthal, Smetana, and Saint-Saens, among others. And without the encouragement he gave to countless musicians, perhaps many of the great romantic compositions would not be in the repertoire today.

When the life of Franz Liszt is measured in terms of all he contributed to others, the extent of his generosity is astounding. Even with all his faults, he is a striking example of a life of consistent benevolence. Rarely has a man been so unselfish toward others, and rarely has a man had such a powerful impact on his times. In the case of Liszt, these two factors are inseparable. His influence continues to be appreciated today, endowing the present generation not only with his own music but also the music of the many musicians he inspired.

Recommended Listening

Orchestral Music: *Les Preludes*; *Faust Symphony*; *Dante Symphony*; piano concerti nos. 1 and 2

Piano Music: Hungarian Rhapsodies; *Liebestraum*; *Annees de Pelerinage*; *Sonata in B Minor*

Organ Music: *Fugue on the Name of B.A.C.H.*

Masses: *Missa Choralis*; *Hungarian Coronation Mass*

Choral Music: *Christus*; *Psalm 13*; *Psalm 116*; *Psalm 128*

"Christianity's
founder was not
wise, but divine....
To believe in Him
meant to emulate
Him: to hope
for redemption,
to strive for union
with Him."

Richard
WAGNER

1813–1883

It is August 1876, and the small Bavarian town of Bayreuth hums with unprecedented activity and anticipation. From all around the world, famous composers, members of the nobility, and devotees of music are gathering, crowding the inns and jostling townspeople in packed cafés. Animated talk all through the town centers on a single subject: a musical premiere and the place where it will be staged.

The event has been long in the making. For the past twenty years, the composer has developed and polished a single work consisting of more than ninety different themes and requiring more than twelve hours to perform. And over the past five years, a massive fundraising effort has finally succeeded in financing an imposing new theater, built exclusively for this composition.

At last, August 13 arrives. Tchaikovsky, Liszt, Saint-Saens, and a host of other composers settle into their seats while members of the aristocracy fill a special "Prince's Gallery." As they await the beginning of the monumental work, members of the audience thumb through an exhaustive "guidebook," attempting to comprehend the scope of the four-opera cycle of music that will be performed over the course of four days.

Members of the orchestra take their places, and the theater falls quiet. A triumphant Richard Wagner exults as the first notes of his magnificent Ring of the Nibelungs fill the concert hall.

Anyone who is acquainted with Richard Wagner's life and work may wonder why he is present in a book about spiritual life. Wasn't he known for his self-centeredness, for pursuing outrageous love affairs, and for befriending the philosopher Nietzsche, the self-styled "anti-christ" and Christian-hater?[1] Wasn't Wagner later idolized by Hitler as a prophet of the Third Reich?[2]

Before closing the book in disgust, wait and see. There is a side of this musical genius that few have ever acknowledged and one that deserves careful consideration. At the same time, there is no excuse for his undeniably shameful actions and views. Approaching an understanding of his life that makes room for some ambivalence does not require us to condone the whole man.

As a boy, the brilliant Wagner showed an early affinity for literature, culture, and different languages, but never for music. Not until he reached his teens—after being inspired by Weber and Beethoven—did young Wagner study music. Then, as he did everything in his life, he rushed into it with reckless abandon. He rushed into marriage as well, proposing to an actress named Minna Planer just after he began his musical career at age twenty.

Wagner and his wife made one another miserable through three decades of dire poverty. Yet through it all Wagner kept on producing musical masterpieces—works that would go unheard and unappreciated for many years. Once, the Vienna Court Opera agreed to produce Wagner's new work *Tristan and Isolde*. Each singer struggled to learn the difficult music, and then struggled further to get through the confusing rehearsals. No one had ever seen such bizarre music, such complexity, such gibberish. Before Wagner could witness the composition's premiere, the opera's frustrated director finally shelved the work as unplayable, after giving it a full seventy-seven rehearsals!

A crucial turning point came in 1864 when one of Wagner's few great admirers, Ludwig II, ascended to the throne in Bavaria and became Wagner's "super-patron." The new king magnanimously paid all of Wagner's debts and gave the composer a generous salary. Now, Wagner's wildest dreams could become reality.

The compositions he created mark the birth of an entirely new genre of musical form, which he called the "music drama." Chief among his accomplishments is the monumental *Ring of the Nibelung* and the mammoth Bayreuth theater built to stage it.

After Wagner's first wife died, he ignited a roaring scandal by wooing the brilliant Cosima Von Bulow, wife of Hans Von Bulow, a noted conductor and devotee of Wagner's music. The Von Bulows' marriage was annulled conveniently, and Wagner married Cosima, which did result in a happy marriage. The composer continued to produce extraordinary works, both in music and literature, until his death at the age of sixty-nine.

Wagner's musical genius stands uncontested, yet his spiritual views form a bewildering assortment of inconsistencies.[3] To begin with, he was a sensitive and impressionable child. He wrote in his autobiography that as a boy he "gazed with agonized sympathy" on the crucifix of his church,[4] and "yearned with ecstatic fervor to hang upon the Cross in place of the Saviour."[5] But the poor examples of his local clergy soon dampened his fervor,[6] and for years the spiritual influences around him were negligible. Yet there are hints of a growing interest in Christianity. Once, he announced he would compose a heroic opera on the life of Martin Luther.[7]

Moreover, the thirty-six-year-old Wagner startled his friends when he embarked on a huge work entitled *Jesus of Nazareth*, saying he was "inspired by a study of the Gospels."[8] His associates flatly discouraged this ambition. Wagner later wrote that the pessimistic philosopher Bakunin, learning of the composer's project, "insisted that I must at all costs make Jesus appear as a weak character."[9] Wagner nevertheless worked for months on the libretto, producing a dramatic harmony of the Gospel accounts.[10] It contained extensive sketches including dozens of other New Testament verses.[11] With no chance of support, the relatively unknown Wagner finally abandoned what could have been an important sacred work.

Still later, he completed a gargantuan work for orchestra and three choruses entitled *The Love Feast of the Twelve Apostles*.[12] The writing displays a clear understanding of the biblical text and perhaps even a measure of devotion to it. Performing the work required 1,200 singers and 100 instruments, and its premiere overwhelmed Wagner himself. He later wrote, "The Holy Ghost was poured out upon my *Love Feast of the Twelve Apostles* and we were all transported."[13]

Christian themes emerge clearly in some of Wagner's music dramas, such as *Tannhauser*, *Lohengren*, and his last great work, *Parzival*, which has been called his "most Christian of works."[14]

As early as 1848, Wagner found himself compelled to address an insistent internal longing for transcendant meaning in life. He wrote, "When I found this yearning could never be stilled by modern life, and realized once again that redemption was to be had only in flight from this life, in escaping from its claims upon me by self-destruction, I came to the primal fount of every modern rendering of this situation—to the man Jesus of Nazareth."[15]

Yet what about his friendship with Nietzsche? It would seem that they were friends only until they really understood one another.[16] In 1876, they met for the last time. Wagner's acceptance of Christianity angered his colleague,[17] who deserted him and later denounced him hysterically in his article, "The Fall of Wagner."[18] Nietzsche wrote, "Incredible, Wagner has turned pious."[19] He bitterly assessed his former friend's conversion by observing, "Richard Wagner, apparently the most complete of victors, fell suddenly, helpless and broken, before the Christian cross."[20]

Wagner's personal faith appeared to be growing. In 1880, he wrote a lengthy article "Religion and Art," in which he calls Jesus Christ, the "all-loving Saviour," who was "born to suffer and die for mankind, redeeming the human race through His blood."[21] Wagner professed belief in the divinity of Jesus,[22] the Virgin Birth,[23] the validity of Christ's miracles, and a literal interpretation of his Second Coming, which he believed would follow the fall of man's political systems.[24]

This composer looked forward to the world's spiritual future: "We await the fulfillment of Christ's pure teaching ... the son of the Galilean carpenter, who preached the reign of universal human love—thus would Jesus have shown us that we all alike are men and brothers."[25]

Wagner wrote that Christ's blood, "was a fountainhead of pity, which streams through the human species."[26] The only hope for the world, Wagner concluded, was the true Christian sacrament, "partaking of the blood of Christ."[27] Concerning Jesus, the composer wrote, "Christianity's founder was not wise, but divine. . . . To believe in him, meant to emulate him: to hope for redemption, to strive for union with him."[28]

Is it surprising to read these quotes? Unfortunately, they tell only half the story. In fact, if Beethoven's Christianity could be considered "unorthodox," Wagner's interpretation is far more so. He utterly rejected the Old Testament, stating that "The Christian God has been erroneously identified with the Jewish tribal god: the god of punishment and war, not the redeeming Saviour of the poor."[29] He dismisses the Ten Commandments as lacking any trace of Christian love.[30]

Many of Wagner's religious views seem to be colored by his apparent anti-Semitic feelings.[31] These odious views were influenced strongly by his associates, especially the French philosopher Count Gobineau.[32] Perhaps this aspect of Wagner's life has been exaggerated in this century in reaction against Adolf Hitler's devotion to his music. Hitler was a vile maniac and a thoroughly unartistic man who neither understood Wagner nor his music.[33] Actually, Wagner surrounded himself with Jewish friends and supporters, notably Rubinstein, Neumann, and his superb conductor, Levi.[34] Wagner urged his conductor and friend to be baptized into the Christian faith, yet he openly admired the man's conviction for remaining steadfast in his Judaism.[35] In a letter to his father, a rabbi, Levi defends Wagner against the charge of anti-Semitism. Levi speaks warmly of their mutual love and admiration.[36]

The great irony of Wagner's peculiar and inconsistent views about Christianity, of course, is that his acknowledged Savior was a Jewish carpenter sent to the lost sheep of Israel. This presented no problem for Wagner. With the sure conviction of the self-deluded, he swept history aside and wrote, "It is more than doubtful if Jesus himself was of Jewish extraction."[37] He made the baffling "discovery" that Jesus was born "among the silent vegetarian communities founded by Pythagoras."[38] Vegetarianism was another one of Wagner's favorite hobbyhorses. For instance, he claimed to have discovered that the Last Supper was an exhortation to vegetarianism,[39] mistranslating Jesus' words: "Taste such alone, in memory of me."[40]

These and many other bizarre ideas leave one wondering whether this musical genius was otherwise mentally deficient.

Was Wagner a Christian? He would have insisted upon it indignantly, at least at some points in his life. But there are few Christians who would not be repelled by his outlandish and unsupportable beliefs. That he had an intense spiritual life cannot be doubted. But the emotions and opinions it produced are, at best, stupefying. The contradictory life of this great composer has bewildered musicologists for decades and continues to do so.

Some Thoughts on Wagner: Perseverance

If ever a man had to persevere singlehandedly through years of relentless failure, it was Wagner. For three solid decades, until Ludwig II came to his rescue, the composer experienced more rejection personally and musically than any other master in written history. Even Handel in England could celebrate an occasional success to balance his array of difficulties. For Wagner, life was an uninterrupted series of defeats, forcing him to move constantly from town to town, but never eliciting surrender.

After failure and rejection from the Thomasschule, he was barely accepted into the University. Soon, his first opera was rejected at Leipzig, and his second was withdrawn after a fiasco in Magdeburg. He was hired as a conductor in Konigsberg, and the company immediately went out of business. Finding another conducting job in Riga, he was soon fired and had to elude frontier guards to escape his creditors. In Paris, a new opera company of his failed, and he actually spent time in a debtor's prison. Finally, he had a "hit" opera (*Rienzi*) in Dresden, but even this proved a financial calamity. Although it brought immediate cash and a good job in Saxony, news of Wagner's success traveled swiftly to his many creditors throughout Europe. They pounced upon him, demanding huge sums of money he still could not pay.

By this time, his marriage was in ruins, debts continued to mount, and he frequently fell ill, needing expensive medical treatments. Wagner's next few operas flopped. Then he narrowly escaped being thrown in jail when he foolishly joined a political rebellion, which forced him to flee into Switzerland. Yet, at a time when he desperately needed to write works that could bring quick money, he was determined to pursue the composing of his mammoth *Ring* cycle. He labored on it tirelessly, fully aware that even if he lived to complete the project, he would surely never have the funds to see it produced.

How could he have kept going? It would seem that Wagner refused to acknowledge the concept "impossible." The defeats he encountered would have crushed the strongest of temperaments, yet he continued to create music that redefined an entire art form. It took years for some of his works to gain acceptance, but now he has an almost cult-like following throughout the world. His music is not for everyone, but those who cherish it are often fanatical zealots who spend a fortune each year flying from around the globe to experience the Bayreuth festivals. It may not always be easy to appreciate his compositions, much less his peculiar beliefs. Yet it is impossible to feel anything but awe for a man of such unshakable perseverance.

Recommended Listening

Orchestral Music: *Siegfried Idyl*
Opera: *Tannhauser; Lohengrin; Tristan und Isolde; Die Meistersinger; The Flying Dutchman; The Ring of the Nibelungs (The Rhinegold, Siegfried, The Valkyries, and The Twilight of the Gods); Parzival*
Choral Music: *The Love Feast of the Twelve Apostles*

"Besides Goodness and Truth, there was Beauty, which proceeded from the other two as the Holy Spirit from the Father and the Son."

Charles
GOUNOD

1818–1893

The young boy's palms were moist and his throat was dry. No thirteen-year-old enjoys being sent to the principal's office.

As the boy hurriedly found a seat, the principal said sternly, "Your mother tells me that you want to leave our school and become a musician. Why do you think you want this?"

"Because," he stammered, "because I love music."

The principal smiled. "Perhaps you do not realize what a hard life a musician can have."

Now the boy was gaining confidence. "That makes no difference," he replied.

"Then give me some proof of your talent." The principal's smile faded as he pulled two pieces of paper from a drawer and handed them to the boy. "Here is a poem, and here is some music paper. See if you can set this to music."

To the principal's amazement, the boy glanced at the poem and immediately began to write a melody. He vaulted to the nearby piano and, improvising an accompaniment, sang the entire poem. As he played the final chord, the young Charles Gounod beamed at his dumfounded principal, who mumbled, "You are right. You will be a musician."

The boy who would one day astound the musical world with his great opera *Faust* was born in Paris' Rue de l'Eperon on June

17, 1818. Gounod's father, a successful painter and lithographer, died when the boy was only five. His mother was a remarkable woman, a renowned pianist, an excellent businesswoman (she managed her husband's lithography business after his death), and a fine mother, by her own son's words. In the introduction to "Memoirs," Gounod would remember in 1877, "My story bears witness to my love and veneration for the being who bestows more love than any other earthly creature—my mother! Maternity is the most perfect reflection of the great Providence; the purest, warmest ray He casts on earthly life; its inexhaustible solicitude is the direct effluence of God's eternal care for His own creatures."

From his earliest days, he had an unquenchable love for music. In his mother's diary, she wrote of her child, "Passionately fond of music in a way I have rarely seen before." Gounod himself later remarked, "If they had attempted to prevent me from learning music, I should have run away to America and hidden in some corner where I could have studied undisturbed."

Madame Gounod was also a pious woman,[1] who taught her son the Catholic faith from his earliest days. All his life he remained deeply religious, and his music career was often eclipsed by his desired to enter the ministry. This conflict began in earnest while Charles was in his early twenties. After entering the Paris Conservatory at the age of eighteen, he had won the coveted *Prix de Rome*. His visit to the Eternal City overwhelmed the young man, and his spiritual predisposition was greatly reinforced by a number of new acquaintances.[2]

One of his principal mentors at this time was a Dominican friar and orator named Lacordaire. He was a disciple of Lamennais, the impassioned priest whose aim was to rejuvenate the Catholic faith by a return to basic truths.[3] As Gounod's biographer James Harding, wrote, "Gounod was one of several who listened to the voice of the persuader and joyfully entered the fold."[4]

Finally, he became a member of an association entitled the "Brotherhood of Saint John the Evangelist," composed of young men from the best Roman families; several among these had already abandoned their career in order to enter into holy orders.[5]

It would seem that Gounod would do the same.[6] A letter from Fancy Hensel (Felix Mendelssohn's sister), who was visiting in Rome, speaks of "the religious exaltation of Gounod."[7]

Another great influence on Gounod at this time was a theologian named Charles Guy. We have an extract from a letter Guy wrote the young musician while at Rome: "I know thy soul well. It is only in God that it will at last find true repose, and blossom into fullest beauty."[8] Such influences were a delight to the heavenly minded young Gounod, whose letters home now exhorted his own mother to go further in her devotion and zeal for God.[9]

Although his mother was herself a believer, she was convinced that her son would best glorify God as a musician rather than as a priest.[10] Knowing Charles to be impressionable and quixotic, her letters counseled prudence and moderation.[11] Both sides accomplished their desired effect on the other: His mother became even more zealous in her faith, and Gounod gave up the Brotherhood of Saint John the Evangelist to remain a musician.[12] His mentor, Charles Guy, delighted with both results, assured Gounod that his prayer, "had ascended to God and come down again on your mother in a dew of grace and blessing."[13]

While Gounod was in Rome, his mother had arranged for her son to be appointed organist and musical director at the Eglise des Missions etrangeres in Paris.[14] He delighted to be back home and exhilarated in his mother's many Christian activities. She studied theology with Gounod's friend Charles Guy, who now lived in the same Parisian apartment building.[15] She was constantly visiting the poor, sewing clothes for them, and writing spiritual songs.[16]

"Your mother," a friend said to Gounod, "is, for me, a miracle twice over; I don't know how she finds the time for all her activities, nor where she finds the money she gives to charity."[17]

Gounod spent five years as the music director of his church, and it was one of the happiest times of his life. During this period he again felt what he later described as "as an inclination to take up the ecclesiastical life."[18] He began signing his name "abbe Ch. Gounod." He took a long retreat for the purpose of prayer, Scripture reading, and meditation.[19]

His first biographer, Marie Anne de Bovet, wrote that Gounod's inclination toward the priesthood had much to do with his desire to minister to needy souls: "To restore Christian peace to a wounded soul, to dispel remorse by divine forgiveness, and soothe the anguish of repentant sinners, seemed to him the most sublime missions to which a human being could aspire, and he prepared himself for holy orders."[20]

Finally, in the fall of 1847, the Archbishop of Paris permitted him permission to attend the lectures at the Carmelite Seminary of Saint-Sulpice to prepare him for the priesthood.[21] He donned his cassock and might have been forgotten by music history except for an interesting encounter. Gounod met the famous prima donna Pauline Viardot, who was so impressed by the young religious musician that she insisted he write an opera expressly for her.

He composed this first work for the stage, *Sapho*, which introduced him to the Paris Opera Company in 1851. Though he also composed several beautiful masses in this period, notably his profound *Messe Solennelle*,[22] he found his greatest talent to be writing for the stage. He hung up his cassock permanently and married Anna Zimmerman, the daughter of a Paris musician and teacher.

In 1859, he created a work that would put both his love for theology and opera together: *Faust*. Many other composers, before and after, have been inspired to compose pieces based on Goethe's epic tale, but none rivals Gounod's greatest opera. Its plot contains everything from Faust's selling his soul to the devil to the triumphant salvation of Margauerite. It portrays the classic conflict of heaven and hell, but the beautiful melodies of Gounod are what make the opera so breathtaking. After a slow start, *Faust* has become one of the world's most performed and beloved pieces of music.

Other operas would follow, notably his dramatic *Romeo and Juliet*. But only one other work for the stage would have as much spiritual content as *Faust*—his opera *Polyeucte*.[23] The work tells of the struggle between early Christianity and the pagan Roman Empire. One of Gounod's greatest scenes is when Polyeucte reads the Gospel to his wife, Pauline, as she lies in prison. As his narrative builds toward the Crucifixion, the intensity of the music is overwhelming.

Faust and his other operas gave the "Abbe Gounod" great fame. However, his devotees occasionally carried their admiration a bit far. Once, a rich woman of society visited the Gounod home. This admirer happened to notice a cherry stone on the mantel, which she stole and had a jeweler set into a brooch surrounded by pearls and diamonds. Some time later, this woman showed this evidence of her veneration to the composer. Imagine her face when the puzzled Gounod said, "But madam, I never eat cherries. The stone you found on the mantlepiece was from a cherry eaten by my servant Jean!"

Gounod continued to compose in various genres, especially songs. One of his most popular ones is *Nazareth* (originally called *Jesus de Nazareth*), composed in May, 1856.[24] Another piece—or at least "half a piece"—is perhaps his most performed composition: the "Bach-Gounod" *Ave Maria*. He simply wrote a lovely melody using Bach's *Prelude no. 1 in C Major* as its accompaniment.

His two greatest oratorios, *Redemption* and *Mors et Vita*, both reveal different aspects of his devout faith in Christ. The former had occupied the composer, off and on, for fully twelve years.[25] Gounod has preceded the score of what he terms a sacred "trilogy" with a few explanatory words. He describes his work as being the expression of the three great events upon which rest the existence of Christianity: (1) the Passion and death of the Savior, (2) his glorious life on earth between his resurrection and ascension, and (3) the diffusion of Christianity throughout the world by the apostolic mission. These three parts of the "trilogy" are preceded by a prologue on the Creation, the Fall, and the promise of a Redeemer.[26] Gounod took extravagant care in the composition of this work, especially in its lavish orchestration.[27]

Mors et Vita was intended to be the continuation of Gounod's sacred perception.[28] Concerning its subject, Gounod wrote, "Although life precedes death in order of time, in the Eternal order death precedes life. Death is the end of existence, of what dies every day, but it is the initial moment, the birth, of what never dies."[29] The first part consists of a "Requiem," the second is descriptive of the Judgment, and the last deals with eternal life. Hence its title, *Mors et Vita*.[30]

Gounod also wrote a great deal of church music, masses, hymns, a Requiem, and another smaller oratorio, *Tobie*.[31] His faith was constantly enhancing his composition and his teaching. "When Christ entered Jerusalem," he says, developing his theories on sacred music, "and the people on His passage cried out, 'Hosannah! Son of David!' the disciples said unto Him, 'Master, bid them be silent,' but He answered, 'if men are silent, stones will speak'—*Lapides clamabunt*. Well, a choral Mass must symbolize these words; it must be an edifice in stone, austere, grave, massive and solemn."[32]

He was quite open about his Christian convictions. He ended a talk given at the public meeting of the Academie des Beaux Arts with the verse John 3:3, which he called "the supreme formula": "Truly I say to you, except a man be born again he can in no case enter into the kingdom of heaven."[33] Talking to reporters once, he commented, "Besides Goodness and Truth, there was Beauty, which proceeded from the other two as the Holy Spirit from the Father and the Son."[34] Even in Gounod's musical writing, such as his commentary on Mozart's opera *Don Giovanni*, his moral perception is disclosed, as he interprets the wicked main character's deserved judgment.[35]

All of his biographers agree as to Gounod's religious convictions. Marie Anne de Bovet insists, "It is very justly said that he is a believer, and that every one of his religious compositions is a confession of faith. A profound theologian, a learned student of Holy Writ and of the Fathers of the Church, he could as readily write a sermon as an opera."[36] Ellen Orr wrote that "Gounod was a Christian as well through his intelligence as through his heart, and was possessed of no less faith than love."[37] Henry Tolhurst summarized the consensus of history when he concluded, "Truly, the Church lost a brilliant servant in him."[38]

Though Gounod spent much of his life in the service of the Catholic Church, his faith reached out beyond denominational barriers. When asked about this subject, he readily asserted, "If a good Catholic were to dissect me, he would be much surprised at what he would find inside."[39] His early biographer, Marie Anne de Bovet, noted that "while he submits to his country's customs, he approves the etiquette adopted in Protestant countries for the execution of sacred music."[40]

A visit to the Gounod home gave many evidences of his faith. In the center of his large organ was a medallion representing a head of Christ.[41] His bookcases were filled with Bibles and religious books and sermons, including a large sheet on which he grouped, in a wide semicircle, the principal articles of the Christian faith, designing a species of chart, which demonstrates the metaphysical and moral world.[42]

Gounod's faith grew ever more fervent toward the end of his life. In his last year, he gave an interview in which he quoted from the apostle Paul: "For I am now ready to be offered, and the time of my departure is at hand. I have fought a good fight, I have finished my course, I have kept the faith." In this last year, his mind often wandered. Sometimes he would break out with the exclamation: "Holiness!" He struggled for words. "Holiness . . . is a precelestial translucence . . . a foretaste of the immateriality of the future life." He looked up, his eyes at the sky. "God loves those whom He admits into suffering."[43]

On Sunday, October 15, 1893, Gounod was at his piano, quietly singing his *Requiem*. As he reached the "Benedictus" movement, his daughter sang along, to her father's delight. A little while later, the composer sat studying the score. When he did not respond to his wife's call, she came into the room and found him slumped over and in a coma. Two days later, Gounod died, leaving his daughter, a son, and his wife of forty-one years.

Some Thoughts on Gounod: Friendliness

It was said that Gounod wanted to enter the ministry because of his great love for people as well as his devotion to God. Although he remained a layperson, these qualities never left him. Since Gounod spent his life loving his neighbor, he was always surrounded by many appreciative friends. Henry Tolhurst wrote that "Those who knew him best describe him as a good and sincere man . . . a lovable man, a 'gentleman' in the fullest sense."

Gounod clearly valued his friends far more than worldly wealth. An offer of a million francs to go on an American tour did not tempt him to leave those he loved, even temporarily.

He had many friends in the priesthood, as well as a great number of prominent musicians. He was particularly close to Cesar Franck and Jules Massenet, with whom he shared both compositional talents and a kinship of faith.

Gounod's friends included many musicians of the younger generation, whom he helped and encouraged in their careers. He gave Claude Debussy a recommendation that enabled him to find work as an accompanist, and he wrote him many warm letters, telling Debussy, "You have genius, young fellow." He was a continual encouragement to the composers Eduard Lalo, Georges Bizet, Henri Busser, and many others—even when he could not help but disagree with their musical style. He spent hours copying down the melodies of Pierre Dupont, a local folk singer. For his own copyist he insisted on employing an elderly, poverty-stricken musician. Gounod paid him generously and treated him as an equal, welcoming him as an honored guest at his dinner table.

This was a man who had a genuine love of people and an infectious sense of humor. Even strangers who came into contact with him were put at ease by his friendly manner. While walking through Paris once, he heard a street organ grinding out one of his arias at breakneck speed. "Ah, friend," he smiled, "not so fast! Look, let me turn the handle." The street musician was too amused by this stranger to stop him, and as the notes came out at the proper speed, Gounod said gently, "This is the tempo. And let me tell you, my good fellow, I wrote it."

Recommended Listening

Operas: *Faust; Romeo et Juliette; Mireille; Polyeucte*

Choral Music: oratorios, *La Redemption, Mors et Vita,* and *Tobie; Messe Solennelle; Requiem;* cantata, *Fernand*

Songs: *Nazareth; Ave Maria* (melody superimposed on Bach's *Prelude no. 1 in C Major*)

"Don't try to do a great deal, but rather seek to do well."

Cesar
FRANCK

1822–1890

The church of Sainte-Clotilde was dark and shadowy after the brightness of the Paris streets. A small group of music students had gathered to hear their teacher improvise on the organ. They all considered the man to be rather curious, absent-minded, and eccentric. But when he played the organ they held him in highest awe.

Suddenly the door opened and an elderly man in a black cassock entered. An old priest, coming to hear the organist play? He was ignored by the students, until one of them happened to get a good look at his face. The youthful mouth dropped and he gasped to his friends, "It is Liszt!" The greatest pianist in the world had also come to hear their organ teacher.

Liszt insisted upon hearing some of the organist's own compositions and would not be deterred by a profusion of modest protests. Finally, the man agreed to perform his Six Pieces for organ. As the music filled the church, Liszt was visibly moved. When it was time for him to leave, the aging master descended the organ loft muttering that J. S. Bach must have returned to life. It was an apt metaphor for composer-organist Cesar Franck, who spent most of his life writing music for the glory of God.

Cesar Franck was a man from another time. Living in Paris during revolutions and protests, he contentedly went about his business teaching and writing music. Surrounded by strongly opinionated French musicians, he modestly kept his views from interfering with his many friendships. While his contemporaries fought for the public's attention, he was not even aware of the tumult. In fact, the day he married was during the 1848 rebellion in Paris, and the happy couple had to climb over a barricade to enter the church—Franck seemed hardly to notice.

This quiet composer was actually a disappointment to his music-loving father, who insisted that his talented son pursue the exciting career of a virtuoso pianist. As a young man, Franck showed that he had the fingers of a Mozartian prodigy, but not the temperament. At the Paris Conservatoire, he was drawn much more to the organ and to composition.

But his father's dream wasn't dead yet. He removed his son from the Conservatoire and set up several recitals, including one for the King of Belgium. Yet a piano career simply did not suit Cesar Franck, and soon he was back in Paris. He had a deeply religious character, and his first major composition was an oratorio entitled *Ruth*.

Soon after this, Franck married, and his semimusical wife Felicite became both a support and a critic. For several years she enjoyed listening to his music and copying his scores. But as his compositions advanced in complexity, she often objected. Their granddaughter told a story of Mrs. Franck in a room adjacent to the composer at work: "If his music tickled her fancy, she could not resist coming into the room to listen to it at a closer hearing; but if the Master poured out sounds that seemed to her too complex or bold, she would throw open the dividing door and call to him: 'Cesar, I do not at all approve of that piece you are playing!'"

In 1872, he took a position as organ professor at the Paris Conservatoire. His many students included some of the finest in France's next generation: Debussy, Duparc, D'Indy, and Chausson. His teaching was as inspirational as tutorial. One student remembers several repeated statements of his instructor: "Don't try to do a great deal, but rather seek to do *well*"; "no matter if only a little can be produced"; "bring me the results of *many* trials, which you can honestly say represent the very best you can do"; "don't think that you will learn from my correction of faults *of which you are aware*, unless you have strained every effort yourself to amend them."[1]

His students loved and admired this kindly man but knew him to be more than a little eccentric. Franck would frequently interrupt his teaching—even mid sentence!—to run to his music paper and jot down a few new measures that had just occurred to him. Then he would continue the lesson precisely where he had left off as if nothing had happened, to the marvel and amusement of his pupils.

One student, Vincent D'Indy, gives us a reliable picture of Cesar Franck: "Physically Franck was short, with a fine forehead and a vivacious and honest expression, although his eyes were almost concealed under his bushy eyebrows; his nose was rather large, and his chin receded below a wide and extraordinarily expressive mouth. His face was round, and thick grey side-whiskers added to its width. Such was the outward appearance of the man we honoured and loved for twenty years; and—except for the increasing whiteness of his hair—he never altered till the day of his death."

His generous nature left no room for any jealousy of fellow musicians. He constantly admired the music of Liszt, as well as Chopin, who was his pianist rival in Paris. Franck spoke openly in praise of Massenet's music, and even respected the musical experiments of the young Claude Debussy. A classic example of Franck's magnanimity was his public applause for Saint-Saens' music, since this praise was far from reciprocal. Even though this composer openly disparaged Franck, there are dedications of his music to his "friend Camille Saint-Saens."

He was also known for his hospitality and liked to welcome his friends and students at any hour. They universally cherished his paternal affection, calling him "Father Franck."

His humility was legendary, and he was careful not to take his opinions too seriously—even those concerning his own compositions. Vincent D'Indy recalls, "When he was hesitating over the choice of this or that tonal relation or over the progress of any development, he always liked to consult his pupils, to share with them his doubts and to ask their opinions."

Once, he astonished a fellow musician by his modesty and deference. Showing the conductor Sylvain Dupuis two different drafts of a composition, Franck asked, "Which do you prefer?" The amazed Dupuis—more accustomed to opinionated composers who would never dream of such a question—quietly gave his choice. Franck announced, "That's settled! I will adopt your view!"

Like Bach, whom he loved and venerated, Franck was much more known as an organist than a composer during his lifetime. For over thirty years he served as organist at Sainte-Clotilde, faithfully playing hundreds of Sundays and Feast Days. Yet this busy schedule, which included a great deal of teaching, never deterred him from composition.

Franck's unassuming and reserved personality disinclined him to put many of his feelings on paper; thus, we have very few of his own words concerning his faith. Fortunately, the warmth of that same personality brought him many close friends and admiring students, many of whom later wrote their recollections of Cesar Franck. It is through these acquaintances, and the biographers who have recorded their words, that the portrait of a devout Christian man emerges.

His student and fellow composer, Vincent d'Indy, was Franck's first biographer. Having worked together for many years, D'Indy found that Franck's "untiring force and inexhaustible kindness were drawn from the wellspring of his faith; for Franck was an ardent believer. With him as with all the really great men, faith in his art was blended with faith in God, the source of all art."[2] He wrote that, "whether he played for some chosen guest, for his pupils, or for the devout worshippers during service, Franck's improvisations were equally thoughtful and careful, for he did not play in order to be heard, but to do his best for God and his conscience' sake."[3]

Another musician who knew Franck well was Charles Bordes, who objected to the ultra-Catholic portrait of Franck painted by D'Indy: "Franck was indeed a *Christian artist*, but more Evangelical than really Catholic, whatever Mr. D'Indy may say, for the latter firmly presents us with the image of an artist of profound faith. Faith Franck certainly had, but he was above all things Evangelical, and the Jesus who sang to him was rather the Jesus of the first centuries of the Christian Church than the Christ of Catholic doctrine."[4]

Still another musician who remembered Franck was M. Guy Ropartz, who wrote, "He was deeply religious but in no way bigoted. I never heard him say anything unkind about anyone and never a bitter word on the subject of the neglect of his works."[5]

Biographers are agreed as to the importance faith played in Franck's life. Taking Franck's cantatas as an example, Lawrence Davies wrote, "Franck's purpose in writing sacred cantatas was accordingly not so much to comfort the believer as to arouse the potential convert."[6] Norman Demuth concluded, "Franck practiced what he believed out of church as well as in it. The Christian tenet 'Love thy neighbor' was a command that he obeyed by instinct. He loved the Lord his God because he knew that his gifts sprung from Him."[7] Another biographer, Hendrik Andriessen, noted that Franck, "was in every period of his life naturally attracted by the beauty of Biblical imagery."[8] And the musicologist Alfred Einstein stated that his works do not rest in faith; they effect a "deliverance into faith."[9]

Perhaps the best way we can see Franck's faith in action is through the magnitude of his own sacred compositions. He wrote a great deal of music using Scripture as his text, from solo songs to biblical scenes with orchestra, such as his *Ruth* and *Rebecca*. But his major works in this genre were his cantata *Redemption*, and the oratorios *The Tower of Babel* and *The Beatitudes*.

Redemption is a three-part oratorio embracing virtually all of history. Part 1 begins with the origins of sinful man, and ends with the announcement of Christ's birth. Part 2 is a symphonic interlude, portraying symbolically: "Centuries pass. The joy of the world transformed and flourishing by the word of Christ. The era of persecution is started in vain, Faith triumphs over all obstacles. But now the modern period has come! Belief has perished, and mankind, once more possessed by a cruel lust of enjoyment, and vain agitations, returns to the passions of the earlier ages."[10] Finally, the text of part 3 proclaims the need for believers to repent and to pray, culminating in the redemption of those who put their trust in God.

In *The Tower of Babel*, the composer does more than simply portray the biblical story. He uses the dialogue between God and man to create, as one biographer put it, a "proselytizing dialogue in which God and Humanity are brought face to face."[11] Sadly, Franck never published this work in his lifetime, and it was not well known until long after his death.

Perhaps Franck's greatest sacred work is his nine-section oratorio, *The Beatitudes*. His student and friend Vincent D'Indy tells us that "all through his life Franck had desired to write a musical work on that beautiful chapter of the Gospels, *The Sermon on the Mount*."[12] He spent the decade between 1869 and 1879 on the score, and its beauties are evident even on first hearing. The dramatic way in which Franck conveys the words of Christ led one biographer to state, "In *Les Beatitudes* Franck preached a gospel which he wished the world would adopt."[13]

Though the world by and large would neither adopt his beliefs nor immediately embrace his music, Franck continued to compose almost to his dying day. Certainly he considered it his duty before the Lord, as much as his weekly duties as organist at Sainte-Clotilde. One can almost see him in his organ loft as he would stop midway through an improvisation and quietly kneel to pray.[14]

Some Thoughts on Franck: Serenity

In a day when professionals never cease from their striving to "get ahead," it is refreshing to find a world-class talent who seemed to rise above it all. Throughout his life, Franck had a serene and contented countenance, which was undisturbed by success or failure. It was said that the finding of a single new chord was adequate to keep him happy the rest of the day. His student and friend D'Indy remembered, "He aimed only at expressing his thoughts and feelings by means of his art, for, above all, he was a truly modest man. He never suffered from the feverish ambition that consumes the life of so many artists in the race for worldly honour and distinction."

Even when his compositions were maligned by the public, Franck was unruffled. The first performance of his *Symphony in D Minor*—now a classic in every orchestra's repertoire—was a complete disaster. In spite of the many criticisms of those present, Franck was delighted at the premiere. One of his students, Pierre de Breville, writes, "Going out we trembled to find Father Franck saddened by the coldness of the public. He was radiant." After the event, when he met his wife (who could not be present), she peppered him with questions. Did the performance go well? Did the audience like the work? Was there plenty of applause? To which "Father" Franck, thinking only of the music itself, replied with a beaming countenance: "Oh, it sounded well, just as I thought it would!"

He seemed completely satisfied after the premiere of *Redemption* was bungled in 1873. He showed the same equal temper when the third and eighth *Beatitudes* were botched by the orchestra during a festival in 1887. Franck found pleasure in taking the long-term view. "Of one thing I am certain," he told his wife, Felicite, at the end of the evening, "it is a very fine work."

This compliant attitude about his music did not stem from a lack of confidence or a languorous lifestyle. Franck was a hard worker, who was composing by five-thirty every morning of the year. His son George testified, "My father was the incarnation of life itself—always active and ebullient. His nervous energy was immense, and was controlled only by clear thinking and instant will-power."

Franck's secret was an inner knowledge of the true judge of his music, his Lord and Savior. He worked in his service alone, without the need for praise from men to give him encouragement. His abiding serenity was founded on his steadfast faith, and it enabled him to create masterpieces without a thought to their failure or success in the eyes of men.

Recommended Listening

Orchestra Music: *Symphony in D Minor*; *Symphonic Variations* for Piano and Orchestra

Chamber Music: *String Quartet in D Major*; *Piano Quintet in F Minor*; *Sonata in A Major* for violin and piano

Choral Music: *The Beatitudes*; *Redemption*; *Ruth*; *The Tower of Babel*

Keyboard Music: *Prelude*; *Aria and Finale* for piano; *Three Chorales* for organ

"Sometime I will have to give an account of myself. How would the Father in Heaven judge me if I followed others and not Him?"

Anton
BRUCKNER

1824–1896

As soon as the orchestra began to play, everyone in the Viennese audience could sense something was wrong. This concert, a symphony conducted by its composer, was not going over very well. At first the audience began murmuring, but soon loud jeers were heard. A contingent of faculty from the Vienna Music Conservatory burst into laughter. Finally, people were sneaking from their seats. The trickle grew and grew until the audience was leaving in droves. By the time the music was over, the large concert hall held but twenty-five listeners.

The composer of this innovative symphony had been so absorbed in his music that he was oblivious to the audience's protests. Wringing with sweat from his labors, he set down the baton and turned to receive his applause. In stunned horror, he saw the hundreds of empty seats where his audience had been.

Tears came to his eyes. He seemed in a stupor, unable to budge. After an awkward time, the embarrassed orchestra members stole from the stage. Of the twenty-five who had remained in the audience, one was the young composer, Gustav Mahler, who came to the podium to express his esteem for the music. But the conductor still could not move. Finally, he stammered, "Let me go. The people do not want to know anything of me." It would still be many years before the Viennese musical society would appreciate the genius of Anton Bruckner.

The little country of Austria has produced many of the world's greatest musicians, often from the most humble beginnings. Although their lives only overlapped a few years, the composers Schubert and Bruckner have a number of similarities. Both came from a family of schoolteachers and were trained to follow that trade. Neither married, and both lived most of their lives in musical obscurity.

But unlike the short-lived Schubert, Anton Bruckner would be given a long life. He would live to see his music acclaimed by the world, and his genius appreciated and honored. Yet these honors would not come until his later years. For decades before then, he would face more continuous rejection than almost any other composer in history.

Born in a small village of Upper Austria, young Bruckner's musical talent was soon obvious. Encouraged by his music-loving parents, he played the violin at the age of four and by ten was playing organ for local church services. When his father died in 1837, the boy entered the music school at the ancient monastery of Saint Florian. After graduation, Bruckner had a brief stint as a village teacher (his official duties included ringing the town bell at 4:00 A.M. and helping harvest crops in nearby fields!), and was paid the minuscule salary of one dollar per month. But in 1845 he joined the music faculty of Saint Florian's and was able to devote his time exclusively to music.

This baroque monastery and its worshipful atmosphere played a major part in shaping Bruckner's life. When, later in life, the hectic pace of living in a big city would stifle his imagination, he would retreat to the peacefulness of Saint Florian. His pious nature, evident from birth, was nurtured in its ancient walls. At a young age, he was called out from among the village boys for a special blessing by a dying priest. Musically, such surroundings helped him to become a virtuoso on the church's great organ and a lifetime composer of sacred music.

In 1856, Bruckner accepted a position of organist at the Linz Cathedral, where he remained for twelve years. He continued to compose, mostly for chorus and orchestra, his favorite idiom. An important influence on his composing was his introduction to the music of Richard Wagner. He loved the ultrachromatic language of Wagner, and such modernization soon found its way into Bruckner's church compositions. The two composers met, and Bruckner was delighted at the encouragement he was given by the famous Wagner.

Toward the end of his stay in Linz, a combination of overwork and loneliness contributed to a nervous collapse. Perhaps this was also aggravated by his lack of success at wooing a mate. Like Beethoven a few decades earlier, the kindly but rather absent-minded Bruckner was rejected by several young women. He was eventually admitted to a sanitarium for a few months, and its rest-fulness restored his soul. He wrote a friend, "God be praised! He has saved me in time."[1]

The famed Vienna Conservatorium offered him a post in 1868, and when he moved there he unexpectedly found himself in the middle of a musical war. Many in the town—including pow-erful music critics such as Eduard Hanslick—supported the com-poser Brahms as the successor of Beethoven's mantle. Others were in the Wagner camp, and the two sides seemed irreconcilable.

Since Bruckner was such an admirer of Wagner, he was con-sidered a musical enemy by Hanslick, his newspaper, and his many allies. It became nearly impossible to have his works performed. The Vienna Philharmonic performed his *Symphony no. 1*, but it received such a cold response that they refused to play Bruckner's other works. He was told that his *Mass in F Minor* was "unsingable"; again, no performance. Whenever a piece was actu-ally played, Hanslick was waiting to attack with his malevolent reviews. Another critic called Bruckner a "fool and a half."

This lasted for more than a decade, yet Bruckner continued to compose, believing that his talent was a trust given by God. He once explained with deep emotion, "They want me to write in a different way. I could, but I must not. Out of thousands I was given this talent by God, only I. Sometime I will have to give an account of myself. How would the Father in Heaven judge me if I followed others and not Him?"[2]

Eventually, musicians of note began to recognize this persistent composer. When Hans Richter conducted Bruckner's *Symphony no. 4* in 1881, both audience and critics extolled the work. When his *Symphony no. 7* was premiered a few years later, it seemed that all of Europe exploded with approval. Though he was happy that his perseverance had been rewarded, he must have wondered when he read a favorable critic's words: "We asked ourselves in amazement, 'How is it possible that he could have remained so long unknown to us?'"

From then until his death in 1896, Bruckner was more and more respected and honored. He was awarded an imperial insignia by Emperor Franz Joseph, who was ready to bestow upon Bruckner whatever he asked, even a royal pension. The composer's answer to this royal boon? Bruckner asked the Emperor to stop Hanslick from continuing his wretched reviews!

The steadfast faith of Anton Bruckner was the one constant in his life of ups and downs. Biographer Hans Ferdinand Redlich has testified that "Bruckner is perhaps the only great composer of his century whose entire musical output is determined by his religious faith."[3] Another wrote "Religiosity was the center of his heart. He was seeking God in his music. God Himself was his goal."[4] Still another notes, "There was neither a spectacular conversion nor, at any time of his life, a religious crisis. His whole being shows a personality quietly in contact with God. His faith was an entirely unsentimental, firm and masculine belief."[5]

Bruckner considered his compositions to be divinely inspired. He listened to the "voice from within"[6] and looked to God, "whose praises he sang in every note of his music."[7] Bruckner had a strong "conviction that *only he who believes and trusts* finds true peace and the glory of the Lord."[8] Working on his last symphony, he told his doctor that he intended to dedicate it, "to the King of kings, our Lord—and I hope that he will grant me enough time to complete it!"[9] Finally he shortened the dedication to simply "to the good Lord," adding with meekness, "if He will accept it."[10]

Since Bruckner's nine symphonies are so frequently performed today, many orchestral devotees do not realize the greater extent of his sacred music, especially his beautiful masses. Yet even his symphonies, with their many chorales and hymn-like sonorities, have a spiritual quality that is recognized by listeners of many faiths. A devout Catholic, he had many friends of various denominations. As biographer Dika Newlin has pointed out, "a narrowly Catholic religious interpretation would have been quite foreign to his spirit."[11]

Bruckner was known to be a man of prayer and fasting,[12] even keeping an account of his prayers in his diary.[13] If he were to perform on the organ, he would not mount the bench until he had knelt and prayed.[14] Concerning Bruckner's prayers, biographer Hans Ferdinand Redlich has noted, "by all accounts this was no mere word-saying but a complete immersion in a meditative process which took him beyond the confines of the physical world."[15]

Having begun the habit in childhood, Bruckner always stopped to pray whenever he heard a church bell. Often, while he was teaching, a distant bell would ring, and his students remembered that "in the middle of a lesson they suddenly became aware that his mind and spirit were no longer with them: the church bells had rung, and Bruckner was praying."[16] Bruckner's prayerful attitude during his solitary walks led Paul Rosenfeld to comment, "No brother in blank Carthusian aisles could have paced sunken further in prayerfulness, God-passionateness and Lenten mood, than Bruckner through the city roads. There was the father in heaven."[17]

His students remember humorous methods in which Bruckner's biblical training found its way to his music theory classes. He began the first assignment by writing one note on the blackboard, saying: "First God made Adam." Then he added another note a perfect fifth higher and went on: "He soon gave him Eve, and the two did not remain alone."[18] But he made his students study hard, insisting on high standards, both in their work and in their morals. Setting the example, he would "not tolerate anything of a lewd or obscene nature, and whenever the joking or the general conversation tended in that direction, he would either put a stop to it or else take his leave in an ostentatious manner."[19]

Bruckner's faith was reflected in his day-to-day life. He was kindhearted and generous, always bringing bags of sweets in his massive pockets for the choirboys whenever he had a rehearsal.[20] He was modest to the point of true gentleness and always showed sincere gratitude toward those who helped him.[21] His quiet demeanor kept his unashamed convictions from ever appearing offensive to others. A story is remembered in which the composer noticed a Jewish student sitting in the hall during one of his lectures. Bruckner went to him, gently placing a hand on his head and opening a conversation with the inquiry: "Do you really believe that the Messiah has not yet come?"[22]

As he approached his last years, Bruckner's faith never failed him. In a letter written to his former tutor, he mentioned his failing health, but concluded, "It is all as God wills."[23] As he continued to compose his ninth and final symphony, he jokingly told Gustav Mahler, "I must at least finish, or I'll cut a poor figure when I appear soon before the good Lord and he says, 'Well, my boy, why did I give you so much talent if not to sing to my honor and glory? You have not done nearly enough with it!'"[24]

On January 12, 1896, he attended his last performance of his music, that of his beautiful *Te Deum*, one of his favorite compositions. He once used this work to illustrate how he believed his talents were to be used for the Lord. "When God calls me to Him and asks me, 'Where is the talent which I have given you?' Then I shall hold out the rolled up manuscript of my *Te Deum* and I know He will be a compassionate judge."[25]

Anton Bruckner went home to be with his beloved God on October 11, 1896. In accordance with his wishes, he was buried under the powerful organ at the Saint Florian monastery, where he had so often communed through music with the Lord of his life.[26]

Some Thoughts on Bruckner: Meekness

Jesus told his disciples, "Blessed are the meek, for they will inherit the earth" (Matt. 5:5). Yet the virtue of meekness is hard to find among peoples of any epoch, and is not especially exemplified by history's composers. Perhaps composers work with such intensity to "put themselves into the music" that it is difficult to not fight back when their compositions are criticized. But this very quality allowed Anton Bruckner to rise above his critics and outlast them all.

Few composers have ever faced such long-term opposition from a hostile public. A Director of the Vienna Conservatorium told Bruckner to give up on trying to compose and to throw his symphonies into a trash can. When Bruckner dedicated his third symphony to his mentor Wagner, the anti-Wagnerites of Vienna assaulted with wrath, led by Hanslick, who called the symphony "insatiable rhetoric." The work had been accepted by the Vienna Philharmonic but rejected after the first rehearsal. All the musicians except one refused to play the piece.

Yet the composer refused to attack in kind. Instead, he continued to compose work after work, believing that his efforts would eventually be blessed. He even used his own meager resources to give his compositions a hearing. He paid the Vienna Philharmonic eight months of his salary to perform his *Mass in F Minor*, and spent even more for a performance of his *Symphony no. 2*.

His motive for such financial sacrifices was not egotistical, not simply to hear his music performed. Rather, it was his best long-term answer to his many critics. He so firmly believed that God wanted him to compose that he could neither desist nor waste time in meaningless verbal battles with his detractors.

In time, he was rewarded for such meekness. The public came eventually to love his great works and even to scorn those who disagreed. In fact, at the premiere of his *Symphony no. 8*, the audience actually booed his old nemesis Hanslick and sent him scampering out of the concert hall! God had honored Bruckner for his refusing to retaliate against unjust attack. His country came to love this gentle, meek man—and on his seventieth birthday all of Austria celebrated.

Recommended Listening

Orchestral Music: 9 symphonies, notably *Symphony no. 4 in E-flat Major* ("Romantic"); *Symphony no. 7 in E Major*

Choral Music: 3 masses, notably *Mass in F Minor* and *Te Deum*

Chamber Music: *String Quartet in C Minor; String Quintet in F Major*

Keyboard Music: *Fantasy in G Major* for piano; *Prelude and Fugue in C Minor* for organ

"In my study I can lay my hand on my Bible even in the dark."

Johannes
BRAHMS

1833–1897

   The old tavern did not seem like a very respectable place for two of Vienna's most notable musicians to meet. But it was warm, and thankfully a table was free that was far enough from the door to avoid the wind and snow that blew in with every new-comer. Sitting down, the old composer and the music critic both looked forward to a hot meal and a quiet discussion.

   Suddenly the door admitted a number of boisterous young people, whose uproar quickly took over the tavern. The music critic gave a contemptuous glance at this scene, but his scorn soon turned to outrage as a lady from this loud group bounded toward their table. To his astonishment, she seemed to recognize his composer friend, and called out, "Professor! Look, the professor is here! Please, professor, play us some dance music. We want to dance!"

   While the horrified music critic watched in amazement, his old friend rose from the table and walked slowly toward the tavern's untuned piano. His audience shrieked with delight as he began to play waltzes and quadrilles, and the dancing went on for over an hour. Finally, the exhausted pianist excused himself to wild applause, and rejoined his friend, who was too bewildered to speak.

   The scene of this eminent composer playing such dance-hall music might not have so surprised the music critic if he had known the poverty-stricken childhood of the "professor." For he had been so poor that as a youth he often played for such establishments.

Nor was this pianist ashamed of his performance, for he delighted in bringing a little joy to these young people.

The music critic never forgot his friend's impromptu concert and thought that the tavern's owner should have erected a plaque in memory that would have read: "Brahms played dance music in this pub."

Playing on out-of-tune pianos was nothing new to Johannes Brahms. He was born in the slums of Hamburg, Germany, and grew up in an impoverished family. His father was a mediocre musician, and his mother worked as a seamstress. When Johannes' musical talent was discovered, it was encouraged not toward the composition of great symphonies but to bring in a bit more money. Indeed, his first published pieces were hack arrangements under such pen names as Karl Wurth and G. W. Marks—sold to publishers for a few cents apiece.

His turning point came in 1853, when he went on a performing tour with a violinist named Eduard Remenyi. In these travels he met many great musicians—Franz Liszt, Joseph Joachin, and especially Robert and Clara Schumann—all of whom marveled at Brahms' talents. On October 28 of that year, Schumann wrote a now-famous article in his journal, the *Neue Zeitschrift fur Musik*, praising the young Brahms as "the one who would be chosen to express the exalted spirit of the times in an ideal manner."

He was virtually adopted by the Schumanns, and when Robert Schumann died a few years later, Brahms was a great comfort to the grief-stricken Clara. He delighted in taking care of their many children and generously supported the family for four decades. But to the surprise of many, Clara Schumann and Johannes Brahms never married, for he was a confirmed bachelor. In his lifetime he had several "near-misses," even to the point of being engaged. But his love of freedom and solitude always gave him cold feet at the end. "Fetters," he once explained, "I cannot wear!"

Instead, he devoted his life to music, composing some of history's finest masterpieces. His four symphonies rival even those of

Beethoven for their beauty, popularity, and frequency of performance. His choral music, especially the *German Requiem*, is cherished by every singer. His fascinating chamber music, exquisite songs, and superb piano music form the basis for thousands of recitals today. He conquered every genre of music except opera. When conductor Hans von Bulow included Brahms—along with Bach and Beethoven—in his famous phrase, the musical "three B's," he expressed the consensus of history.

Yet this celebrated composer was a unpretentious man, whose greatest pleasures were taking long walks through Vienna, where he moved in 1862. Even after his music made him quite wealthy, he still wore old suits and brewed his own coffee. As he approached fifty, this world-famous musician grew a long bushy beard for the simple reason that he was tired of shaving and wearing ties!

Brahms was charitably generous with his money, supporting many friends and causes, and caring so little about his fortune that he would often stuff bundles of banknotes in a closet and forget them. He constantly sent gifts of money to needy people, even total strangers about whom he had heard. In letters to his parents he always asked if there was "enough money and to share." Once he sent his father a large bundle of banknotes wrapped in a score to Handel's oratorio *Saul*, with the amusing note attached: "Father dear, if at any time things go badly with you, music is always the best consolation. Only study my old *Saul* attentively; you will find something there that will be of use to you."

His long-standing friend Clara Schumann died in 1896, and while Brahms was attending the funeral he caught a cold that intensified the pain of the liver cancer from which he was suffering. Within a year he, too, would die, but not before one last triumph. One month before his death, he attended a performance of his *Symphony no. 4*. After each of the four movements, the audience burst into applause to acknowledge him. At the symphony's conclusion, the ovations were so enthusiastic that Brahms stood in the artists' box with tears running down his cheeks. He died on

April 3, 1897. A newspaper reported that, "All musical Vienna followed the great man to the grave."

For decades, parallels have been noted between the lives of Beethoven and Brahms: their difficult childhood, their personal eccentricities, their bachelorhood, and, to some degree, their musical styles. Perhaps a new parallel should now be added: their strong but unconventional faith in God.

Brahms was raised by God-fearing parents,[1] but unlike Beethoven, they were Protestant rather than Catholic. As a youth, he developed a love for the Bible and for church music, under the tender care of his Pastor Geffcken at St. Michaelis Lutheran Church.[2] Biographer Walter Niemann confirms that, "Brahms was a convinced and believing member of the Lutheran Protestant Church." But he then adds, "Not as regards dogma, not in the letter, but in the spirit."[3]

This report is echoed by many historians. It seemed that Brahms was a believer but a somewhat unorthodox one.[4] He spoke earnestly about God, believed firmly in the next life but was at a loss to choose between dogmas of the various denominations surrounding him.[5] This lack of certainty was sometimes mistaken for disbelief by those of simple pious faith, such as his friend Antonin Dvořák.

We know that Brahms was a diligent student of Martin Luther's German translation of the Bible, as well as Luther's book *Table-talk*.[6] In his fascinating book, *The Unknown Brahms*, Robert Haven Schauffer, notes that, "The Master's compendious knowledge of Scripture was shown, not only by the excellent texts he compiled for the choral works, but also by certain parodies of Biblical style to be found in his letters."[7]

Brahms' many biographers agree that he was a great lover of the Scriptures.[8] Discussing this with a friend, Brahms once remarked, "People do not even know that we North Germans long for the Bible *every* day and do not let a day go by without it. In my study I can lay my hand on my Bible even in the dark."[9]

Certainly this devotion to Scripture is seen in many of his finest works, particularly in the sublime *German Requiem*. Unlike the typical Latin Requiem Mass of history, Brahms insisted on choosing his own Bible verses, verses that speak of comfort and hope in the life to come.[10] The work intertwines over a dozen passages, which range from the serene Psalms to the prophecies of Isaiah, from the Lord's comforting word at the Last Supper to the glories of the book of Revelation.

Other compositions testify to Brahms' faith in Scripture and in God. His *Triumphlied*—written to celebrate the victory of the Prussian armies in 1870–71, contains a powerful exultation of thankfulness to the Lord.[11] Over the second movement of his *Piano Concerto in D Minor* he inscribed the verse, "Benedictus qui venit in nomine Domini" ("Blessed is he who comes in the name of the Lord").[12] Perhaps the best example of Brahms' use of the Bible is the *Four Serious Songs* of his last years. After the first three deal with the mysteries of life spoken about in Ecclesiates, the final song bursts through with the jubilant love theme of 1 Corinthians 13.[13]

Brahms had friends from many Christian denominations, and as a man of character he would encourage all of them to live up to their personal beliefs. He would sometimes reproach the Roman Catholic servant girl who cleaned his rooms if she missed church on Sunday, admonishing her that members of each communion should live up to their duties.[14]

This was the standard picture of Brahms' faith—steadfast if undogmatic—which has been presented and accepted by musicologists for many years. But in 1955, a new testimony was printed which has puzzled many Brahms enthusiasts. Arthur M. Abell published a book entitled *Talks with Great Composers*, which contained long talks he had with Brahms in 1896 on the subjects of inspiration, religion, and the Bible. Mr. Abell insisted that he waited decades to publish these discussions because Brahms demanded, "I must exact from you your solemn word of honor, that you will not publish what you have heard me say here tonight until fifty years after my death."[15]

This book details every word of the long theological conversations between Abell, Brahms, and the violinist Joseph Joachim.

Much of the conversation seems very plausible and is quite enlightening. Concerning his compositions, Brahms states:

"I will now tell you and our young friend here about my method of communicating with the Infinite, for all truly inspired ideas come from God. Beethoven, who was my ideal, was well aware of this.[16]

"When I feel the urge, I begin by appealing directly to my Maker and I first ask Him the three most important questions pertaining to our life here in this world—whence, wherefore, whither [woher, warum, wohin]?[17]

"Straightaway the ideas flow in upon me, directly from God, and not only do I see distinct themes in my mind's eye, but they are clothed in the right forms, harmonies and orchestration.[18]

"You see, the powers from which all truly great composers like Mozart, Schubert, Bach and Beethoven drew their inspirations is the same power that enabled Jesus to work His miracles.[19]

"I know several young composers who are atheists. I have read their scores, and I assure you, Joseph, that they are doomed to speedy oblivion, because they are utterly lacking in inspiration. Their works are purely cerebral. The great Nazarene knew that law also, and He proclaimed in John 15:4, 'The branch cannot bear fruit of itself, except it abide in the vine.' No atheist has ever been or ever will be a great composer."[20]

In these discussions, Brahms has a great deal to say about Jesus Christ. He affirmed that he believed in Jesus' miracles,[21] claims about himself,[22] and his teachings.[23] He further states: "Jesus was the world's supreme spiritual genius, and He was conscious of appropriating the only true source of power as no one else ever was."[24]

"Now Jesus taught us that God is Spirit, and He also said, 'I and my Father are one' (John 10:30).[25]

"Jesus Himself is very explicit about this, in saying, 'Ask and it shall be given you, seek and ye shall find; knock and it shall be opened unto you.' There would not be so much good music paper wasted in fruitless attempts to compose if those great precepts were better understood."[26]

Throughout the dialogues, Brahms refuted the teaching of Darwin and Huxley because of their absence of an acknowledgment of God's power.[27] He affirmed his belief in eternal life,[28] and in the biblical teaching of heaven and hell, as being the literal places of blessing or condemnation in the next life.[29]

Nevertheless, in many of these conversations, there are difficulties. In them, Brahms intermittently referred to a belief that Jesus' words in John 14:10–12 ("It is the Father, living in me, who is doing his work. . . . anyone who has faith in me will do what I have been doing. He will do even greater things than these")— verses that he says the Orthodox church chose to ignore[30]—"flatly contradict" the well-known words of John 3:16 ("For God so loved the world that he gave his one and only Son, that whoever believes in him shall not perish but have eternal life"), which he declared are not Jesus' actual words but those of the Evangelist.[31]

Furthermore, in this book the composer seems fascinated with various stories he has heard of occult practices, levitation, trances, and other "psychic phenomena."[32] He supposedly considered these activities as being proof that "miracles" truly happen,[33] and that those who perform them fulfill the words of Jesus: "Anyone who has faith in me will do what I have been doing. He will do even greater things than these."[34]

Finally, much of the dialogue seems very unlike anything ever reported by the many other eyewitnesses in Brahms' life—not only in the words themselves but in the style of his conversation. Yet Abell insisted that he had employed a bilingual stenographer to record the three-hour discussion verbatim.[35]

It may be many years before musicologists pass a final verdict on this unique book by Arthur M. Abell. Certainly, he must have had some fascinating conversations with Brahms concerning his faith, and it should not surprise us that the composer had much to say on this subject. Indeed, one can only wish that similar conversations had taken place with every composer in history!

Some Thoughts on Brahms: Modesty

In his book, *Personal Recollections of Brahms*, the composer's friend George Henschel wrote that Brahms, "coveted neither fame nor applause. He was of a very simple, kind, childlike disposition. He loved children, whom—poor or rich—to make happy, was to himself a source of pure happiness." This is a picture of true modesty. Even when Brahms had achieved both fame and wealth—at his death he left an estate valued at more than $100,000, a lot of money in the nineteenth century—this intrinsic humility and simplicity never left his character.

Possessing great genius, Brahms was nevertheless unassuming about the masterpieces he composed. After finishing his magnificent *Symphony no. 4*, he mailed the only existing copy of the score to the conductor Von Bulow in an unregistered, ordinary postal packet. Fortunately, the package arrived safely, but Von Bulow was beside himself at Brahms' nonchalance. "What would we have done had the packet gone astray?" he demanded. Without a moment's thought, Brahms answered simply, "In that case I would have to write the symphony anew."

He seemed to master the art of "putting others first." Rather than seeing other composers as his competition, he found ways of promoting them and praising their works, even in comparison to his own. After playing a beautiful Bach sonata one day, Brahms threw a copy of his own *Sonata* on the floor, saying, "After that, who could play such stuff as this?" He was outspoken in his appreciation for Mendelssohn's music: "I'd give all my compositions if I could have written such a piece as the *Hebrides Overture*." Once, at a dinner in Brahms' honor, his host was about to toast "the health of the greatest composer." But Brahms quickly jumped to his feet, glass in hand, and cried, "Quite right! Here's to Mozart's health!" as he began clicking his glass with everyone present.

Here is a man who comprehended the biblical principle, "Honor one another above yourselves" (Romans 12:10). Brahms knew his abilities, and he chose to use them—but not to boast in them. Instead, his praise went to others, and the approval he freely gave to the composers of his day did much to encourage their talents and creativity. It is no wonder that God has used such a man to bring musical happiness to so many millions even now, a century after his death.

Recommended Listening

Orchestral Music: 4 symphonies; *Variations on a Theme by Haydn;* 2 piano concerti; *Violin Concerto; Concerto for Violin and Cello*

Choral Music: *German Requiem; Alto Rhapsody; Liebeslieder Waltzes; Triumphlied*

Chamber Music: 3 string quartets; 2 string quintets; 2 string sextets; *Clarinet Quintet;* 3 piano trios; 3 piano quartets; *Piano Quintet; Horn Trio;* 3 sonatas for violin; 3 sonatas for cello

Keyboard Music: *Variations on a Theme by Paganini; Variations and Fugue on a Theme of Handel; Hungarian Dances;* intermezzi; rhapsodies; waltzes; capriccios; ballades

Songs: *Wiegenlied* ("Brahms' Lulluby"); *Four Serious Songs; Wie bist du, meine Konigin?; Fifteen Romances from Magelone,* op. 33; *Sapphische Ode*

"I study with the birds, flowers, God and myself."

Antonin
DVOŘÁK

1841–1904

The riotous commotion of New York City bewilders the Bohemian maestro arriving there in 1892. In the three years he spends directing the National Conservatory of Music, he vacillates between exploration and retreat. There are times when he wanders to the railway station, awed by the mammoth steam engines and the rushing, chattering crowds. And there are times when he rejuvenates himself alone in Central Park, tossing bread crumbs to flocks of pigeons and drinking in the all-too-rare sight of trees and grass.

Eager to get in touch with the music of this strange, vibrant country, this composer learns from a black American music student the beauty of Negro spirituals. This music conveys ecstatic joy and deep sorrow so effectively that it brings tears to the maestro's eyes.

In the summertime, he feels extremely homesick for his native Prague. Friends persuade him to take the train to rural Spillville, Iowa, where the composer delights in spending time with a community of fellow Bohemians. There, the variegated sights and sounds of America continue to fascinate him. Sitting outdoors on a summer evening, he listens intently as three Iroquois perform traditional Indian music.

In the rural tranquility of Spillville, the composer takes time to sift all the images and impressions that have bombarded him

*since he arrived. He soon begins work on a new composition. The
result is one of Antonin Dvořák's greatest and most celebrated
symphonies, entitled* From the New World.

Present-day Czechoslovakia was known as Bohemia when
Antonin Dvořák was born there on September 8, 1841. His
parents struggled to make ends meet, and they feared their son's
musical ambitions were a sure ticket to continued poverty. Even
though they loved music and appreciated the boy's phenomenal
talent, they told their crestfallen son that an education in music
was out of the question.

Yet Dvořák dedicated himself to his calling as a musician,
leaving home and working his way through Prague's Organ
School. Each day when he left the school, he faced a difficult challenge: His musical studies were hampered because he could not
afford even to rent a piano, much less buy one. He recalled later
that these were years of "hard study, occasional composing, much
revision, a great deal of thinking, and very little eating." Against
all the odds, Dvořák became—and remains—the greatest composer of his nation's musical history.

In Prague, Dvořák spent time with many talented musicians.
When he was twenty-two, Dvořák played viola in an orchestral
concert of Wagner's music, conducted by the composer. This experience affected him deeply, and for several years his youthful compositions reflected Wagner's influence. But as a composer he
remained virtually self-taught: "I study with the birds, flowers,
God, and myself."[1]

At the beginning of his career Dvořák met the famous composer Johannes Brahms, who became a close friend and strong supporter. Brahms convinced his publisher to distribute Dvořák's
music, and he influenced musicians throughout Europe to play the
young composer's works. By his mid-forties, Dvořák's fame was
well-established. His musical career would span the globe, with
performances from Vienna to Chicago. When he died in 1904, his
native Bohemia declared a day of national mourning.

National and international acclaim did not alter Dvořák's simple and humble nature. In no way did he fit the stereotype of the eccentric composer. He cherished his wife and many children and savored their company even as he composed. Instead of retreating to the solitude of a private study, Dvořák often worked at the kitchen table. Surrounded by the aroma of bread baking in the oven and the din of children chasing noisily through the house, Dvořák did some of his best composing.

A revealing picture of Dvořák's home life is given by a student who recalled, "His children were permitted to invade his studio at all times, even while the composer was at serious work. My daily lessons were usually taken with the accompaniment of grimacing boys and girls hidden behind articles of furniture, or appearing at unexpected moments in doorways out of their father's sight."[2]

Throughout his life, Dvořák maintained a reputation of character, high morals, and great faith.[3] He spoke of his genius as "the gift of God" or as "God's voice."[4] When writing about his colossal *Mass in D Major*, he characteristically proclaimed, "Faith, hope and love to God Almighty and thanks for the great gift of being enabled to bring this work in the praise of the Highest and in the honour of art to a happy conclusion." Then he added, "Do not wonder that I am so religious. An artist who is not—could not produce anything like this. Have we not examples enough in Beethoven, Bach, Raphael and many others?"[5]

Dvořák's relationship to God appears to have been consistently reverent and personal.[6] His principal biographer, Otakar Sourek, notes that an unchanging feature of Dvořák's nature was his "sincere piety."[7] The composer loved reading the Bible and owned copies in English as well as in modern and ancient Czech.[8] Dvořák's letters are full of spiritual observations, and his manuscripts regularly began with the marking "With God" and ended with the benediction, "God be thanked."[9] When he traveled, he wrote letters to his children encouraging them to go to church often and "pray fervently."[10]

Once, while working with a librettist on his opera *Rusalka*, he observed that a character was supposed to say, "I curse both God and spirits all." This troubled Dvořák immediately, and he asserted, "Listen, I am a believer. I can't curse God in my music."[11] When he first met Anton Seidl, conductor of the New York Philharmonic Orchestra, Dvořák was horrified at the man's blasphemous speech and his irreligious beliefs, yet he continued to befriend the conductor.[12] His beloved friend Brahms, though not an agnostic, distressed Dvořák because of his lack of simple faith. A person who listened in on a long conversation about religion between the two composers later noted, "On the way back to the hotel, Dvořák was more than usually silent. At last after some considerable time he exclaimed with emotion, 'Such a man, such a soul—and he doesn't believe in anything, he doesn't believe in anything!'"[13]

He viewed his extraordinary composing skills as being inspired by God, claiming that he would "simply do what God tells me to do."[14] Dvořák's sacred music reveals the portrait of a devout soul. Musicologist Mosco Carner writes, "Religious music was to him a means to express in the first place his feeling of devotion, his idea of the Deity."[15] He sometimes used parts of old Czech hymns and plain-chant melodies,[16] but would often blend the holy texts with lively dance themes from his native Bohemia. As biographer Gervase Hughes aptly notes, "Consequently it was not unnatural that Dvořák should set the opening lines of the 'Credo' to a melody that would have served equally well for a graceful waltz, and having thereafter treated the references to Christ's crucifixion and death in a mood of deep seriousness he saw nothing incongruous in bursting once again into a somewhat perfunctory jog-trot at the word 'et resurrexit.'"[17]

Dvořák's beautiful *Stabat Mater* is considered by many to be his greatest work.[18] The music was set to the poem by Jacopone di Todi, and in it the grief of Jesus' mother echos Dvořák's own grief at the loss, within a short time, of three of his children.[19] His exquisite *Biblical Songs*, based on ten of his favorite psalms, have been called "ten variations on the theme of God."[20] *Saint Ludmila*, Dvořák's dramatic oratorio, celebrates the conversion of the

Czechs to Christianity. During a pagan festival to a goddess, the hermit Ivan shatters her statue and calls upon all present to worship instead the one true God whose Son died upon the cross. He wins the young Princess and her future husband, Borivoj, to Christ, and the work culminates with their joyous baptism into the new faith.[21]

Dvořák created a great deal of sacred music,[22] yet many projects he dreamed of were never realized. He wanted to write oratorios entitled *Nazareth* and *Golgotha*,[23] but could never find suitable librettists.[24] Anyone attempting to compose a *Golgotha*, he concluded, needed an extra measure of self-assurance: he must "have such a head," Dvořák said, and he spread his hands wide.[25] At one point, Dvořák began writing sketches for a choral version of "The Song of Songs." But his conservative and old-fashioned personality overruled, and he abandoned the work; the text seemed to him "too sensual."[26]

Dvořák attended the Bohemian Catholic Church, yet the faith he expressed in his life and his music was nonsectarian. The same Dvořák who wrote a Latin Requiem also depicted his beliefs in his *Hussite Overture*, glorifying the ministry of Czech reformer John Hus.[27] His biographer Sourek concludes, "Dvořák's piety was a piety of the heart, of one who is devoted to God from conviction and not to some particular religious community. Dvořák was convinced to the depths of his being that over the world there watches a higher power which directs everything for the best: and he was devoted to that power with fervor and gratitude."[28]

His faith and his life mirrored one another; both were simple, unpretentious, and steadfast. Even at the height of his fame, Dvořák always kept close to nature and often expressed himself by relating to the world God made.[29] He took frequent breaks from his work to gaze at flocks of pigeons and to feed them. As a child, he was once asked to kneel for prayer. He responded, "I like praying best there at the window when I look out on the green and at the sky."[30] Dvořák's legacy as a great composer is enriched immeasurably by his consistent, childlike faith, untainted by a prosperous life of success and prestige.

Some Thoughts on Dvořák: Adaptability

The young Antonin Dvořák appeared to be thoroughly rustic; a humble, provincial man of the soil, yet he would become a world traveler and an international celebrity. Here was a man raised in poverty in the midst of men whose desperate need to put food on the table took captive any larger dreams or ambitions they might have harbored. Dvořák's own father, a struggling innkeeper, loved music and took pride in his son's talent but opposed his training because it seemed presumptuous to imagine that a musician could keep from starving.

Yet Dvořák traveled around the globe, living in every conceivable setting. Within a decade of his first performances he was a world-famous composer, overwhelmed with commissions for new works. From his humble expectations, he had to adapt to a life of travel, public scrutiny, and the company of thousands of adoring strangers. Of course, he never sought after cosmopolitan life; he would always be ill at ease in large cities and most comfortable in the company of a few good friends in a simple setting.

And the effect of all this acclaim on his personality? There was none. Although he readily accommodated great changes in lifestyle—from rural Bohemia to downtown New York City—he remained the same modest Anton that his friends had always known. Even after he achieved worldwide fame (which continued to amaze him), the renowned Dr. Dvořák still felt shy and uncomfortable around those he considered his social superiors.

Perhaps Dvořák could handle the stress of his flight to fame because he never lost the youthful innocence and vivacity of his childhood. He loved to play games with people of all ages. Even as an adult, he had a boyish passion for trains and ocean liners. He cherished children (especially his own), and had an outdoorsman's love of animals. Once, when two of his acquaintances were discussing Dvořák, one of them complained that all he knew was music. The other friend, better acquainted with the composer, countered, "Did you try talking to him about pigs?"

Ultimately, Dvořák's genuine disposition remained unaffected by changes in status because of the composer's profound love for humankind. Since he delighted more in a good friend than in the luxury of riches, he was able to be flexible in the most foreign surroundings. He was convinced that congenial people were to be found everywhere. From the commoners of Bohemia and Spillville, Iowa, to the sophisticates of London and New York, Dvořák remained the same. He adapted to every situation with good humor, and both his music and his character remained uncorrupted by his universal success.

Recommended Listening

Orchestral Music: 9 symphonies, notably *Symphony no. 9 in E Minor* ("From the New World"); *Slavonic Dances*; *Carnival Overture*; concerti for violin and cello

Chamber music: *Quartet in F Major* ("American"); *Quintet in E-flat major*; *Trio in E Minor* ("Dumky")

Piano Music: *Humoresques*

Songs: *Biblical Songs*

Choral Music: *Requiem*; *Stabat Mater*

Opera: *Saint Ludmila*; *Russalka*

"The Spirit of God is not something less than God, it is God."

Edward

ELGAR

1857–1934

In a small town in England, a young man sat lazily behind the counter in the only music store around for many miles. There were few serious customers in this rural setting, and the store was filled with zithers, accordions, banjos, and mouth organs rather than violins, oboes, or French horns.

Suddenly an older gentleman entered, his baffled expression revealing that he had never been in the store before. Rising to attention, the young clerk introduced himself and found that the stranger was on holiday nearby. The gentleman looked about at the rustic assortment of musical paraphernalia and asked doubtfully, "Do you have any music paper?"

The clerk smiled and, searching through a drawer, brought forth a page of ordinary, twelve-stave paper. His customer's brow furrowed, and he said, "Oh, yes, but I mean paper with twenty or twenty-four staves on a page."

"Oh! you mean scoring-paper," said the young man, obviously impressed at his musical visitor. He began digging through boxes in the back in the store, and finally emerged triumphantly with a brown-paper parcel. It contained exactly what was wanted, and the gentlemen's smile clearly showed his delight and relief.

As the young man bundled up the purchase, he could not conceal his interest in his curious visiter: "Going to try your hand at a bit of scoring, eh?"

"Well," said the gentlemen quietly, "I thought I might try and do something of the sort.

"Ah," said the young man knowingly, "you'll find it a jolly sight harder than you think—you take my word for it!" If only he knew that his customer was Sir Edward Elgar, knighted by King Edward II as the greatest British composer in two centuries.

M usic stores were a part of Elgar's life from the beginning, since his father was the proprietor of one in which the boy spent countless hours. His father was also an excellent musician, playing violin in various orchestras and serving as organist for the Worchester Cathedral. Music was everywhere in young Elgar's life, and his interest and talent was manifest at an early age. Once the boy was found sitting on the riverbank with a pencil and music paper, insisting that he was "trying to write down what the reeds were saying."

Elgar's father may have been a musician, but he wanted no such career for his talented son. Like many other composers throughout history, his parents forbade their son to enter a conservatory. Instead, at the age of sixteen, he was sent to study law in London. Fortunately, this episode did not last long, and he was soon back in Worchester filling a number of musical roles.

In October 1886, he began teaching piano to a Miss Caroline Alice Roberts, eight years his elder. Soon, "there was more to it than music," and they were married in 1889. She was not only Elgar's wife, she was his greatest fan, and spent her life encouraging her husband's talents.

Although Alice was not a trained musician, Elgar would often play sections of works in progress to obtain her critique. He nearly always followed her advice. Once he played her a new work, which she seemed to like—except for the ending. However, nothing derogatory was spoken, and they retired for the evening. The next morning, the composer found a note pinned to the music: "All of it is beautiful and just right, except this ending. Don't you think, dear Edward, that this end is just a little . . . ?" Without further ado, he changed it until both of them were satisfied.

During the first decade of his marriage, Elgar wrote a number of pieces, but it was not until 1899 that his compositions became well known to the musical public. In that year he presented his two greatest works, the *Variations on an Original Theme* (usually called the "Enigma Variations") and *The Dream of Gerontius*. With the success of these compositions, Elgar became the most important English-born composer since Henry Purcell's death in 1695.

The *Enigma Variations* became the first British composition to enter into the standard orchestral repertoire. It is a series of fourteen musical "portraits," which include his wife, a number of his close friends, and finally himself. The composer is said to have inserted a "silent" theme, which is never played but is cryptically hidden within the work. Hundreds of musicians have painstakingly studied the composition and many guesses have been made, but no one has ever definitively identified Elgar's "Enigma" theme.

Even after his fame was widespread, Elgar kept both his modesty and his sense of humor. Once, while walking around London with a friend, he past a street musician playing the *Salut d'Amour*, one of his early compositions. This so enthralled the composer that he astonished the violinist with the gift of half a crown, asking him, "Do you know what you're playing?"

"Yes, it's *Salut d'Amour* by Elgar," the grateful musician replied.

His benefactor smiled and said, "Take this; it's more than Elgar ever made out of it."

The twentieth century brought many musical honors to Elgar. He was commissioned to write the music for Edward VIII's coronation, and later knighted for his contributions to the music of England. He was later made a Baron, and given the appointment of Master of the King's Music. But with his beloved wife's death in 1920, Elgar compositional energies waned. In October of 1933, a malignant, inoperable tumor on his sciatic nerve was detected. He died the following February, and was laid to rest beside his wife, Lady Alice.

Elgar had a reserved personality and did not easily discuss personal issues. In the Edwardian Age in which he lived, it was not customary for British Christians to articulate their faith, however devout they might be. Rather, it was expected that Christians would exhibit their convictions in their life and work, and it is in his music that this composer best demonstrates his faith in Christ.

Elgar's plans were spiritually ambitious. In the words of musicologist Percy M. Young, "It may be seen that Elgar chose to set to music virtually the whole of the New Testament—or at least so much of it as would with music give such total effect."[1] Few artists in all of history have spent so many years of their life using their gifts to enhance the Scriptures, particularly with his huge compositions entitled, *The Apostles* and *The Kingdom*.

Religion had played an essential part of Elgar's life from the beginning.[2] As the son of the cathedral's organist, he spent many hours in the organ loft with his father as he played his music for the Lord's house.[3] Although his father worked for a Catholic Church, his background was that of the Anglican denomination.[4] Thus the Elgar household was a mix of Catholic and Protestant traditions.

We have few glimpses into the teaching of his youth, but there were those around him who encouraged spiritual growth. Long after he was known as the renowned composer of *The Apostles*, Elgar used to enjoy telling about one of his teachers, Francis Reeve, who fired his imagination during a Scripture lesson with the comment: "The Apostles were young men and very poor. Perhaps, before the descent of the Holy Ghost, they were no cleverer than some of you here."[5]

From comments of later years, we know that the huge plans for the New Testament compositions were formed while Edward was still a youth. Concerning his oratorio, *The Apostles*, he says, "I have been thinking it out since boyhood, and have been selecting the words for years, many years."[6] In the preface to the finished score, the composer wrote, "It has long been my wish to compose an oratorio which should embody the Calling of the Apostles, their Teaching (schooling) and their Mission, culminating in the establishment of the Church among the Gentiles."[7]

It would be a long time before Elgar's great plans for a New Testament saga would be realized. Before then, his talents would undertake similar projects with great success. One of them was an oratorio entitled *Lux Christi* (*The Light of Christ*), op. 29, which contains an excellent selection of the sayings of Jesus.[8] Another was *Scenes from the Saga of King Olaf*, op. 30, about this monarch's conversion from paganism to Christianity.[9]

In the same year as his successful *Enigma Variations*, Elgar produced his most popular chorus work, *The Dream of Gerontius*. Based on a poem that Cardinal John Henry Newman wrote in 1865, it dynamically relates the vision of a Christian named Gerontius as he travels from this life to the next. He encounters both angelic choirs and the demons of hell, but is left with the hope of salvation as he faces the final judgment.

One of the reasons for its powerful impact of this work is the stark realism that Elgar uses to convey the spiritual truths he believed. He rejected sentimentality in favor of sincerity. He once wrote, "Look here: I imagined Gerontius to be a man like us, not a priest or a saint, but a *sinner*, a repentant one of course but still no end of a *worldly man* in his life, and now brought to book."[10]

At first, the forceful drama of *Gerontius* was too much for the stately British public. As musicologist Michael Hurd has written, "It was written with utter conviction and deep passion. It scorned the milk-and-water politeness that passed for music in English academic circles. It was operatic in its intensity. It burned with life and vitality."[11] But the work was soon embraced as a masterpiece and is now regarded in England in the same class as Mendelssohn's *Elijah* or even Handel's *Messiah*.

As Elgar's reputation grew, his compositions included many different genres, from songs to orchestra music. But he continually went back to his lifelong dream of placing the New Testament message to music.[12] In the back of his *New Testament*, acquired in 1882, we find the outline for three great oratorios: *I The Apostles, II The Kingdom, III The Judgment, The Saints, The Vision, The*

Throne, The Holy City, The Fulfillment.[13] He discussed this project with many clergymen and read extensively on the subject.[14] Finally, as his biographer Ian Parrott relates, "With his considerable knowledge of the Bible and with much interest in theology at the time, Elgar was ready to compile his own text."[15]

The first part of the massive trilogy, *The Apostles*, appeared in 1903. Three years later, Elgar finished the second New Testament oratorio, *The Kingdom*. These two works are intricately linked. *The Apostles* is about the period when Jesus walked the earth, and closes with his ascension; *The Kingdom* continues the story, telling of the church in Jerusalem.[16]

It was Elgar's intention that the two works be performed on consecutive evenings. Concerning the work's climactic Great Commission, Ian Parrott writes, "Here the apostles, filled with zeal, go out into the world to preach, and the composer's music has the same urgency and exaltation."[17]

Lamentably, Elgar did not complete a third oratorio for his trilogy. Yet many years later, the last theme he ever wrote, was called "The Judgment" and as he gave it to his friend W. H. Reed, he said, "This is the end, Billy."[18] Nevertheless, *The Apostles* and *The Kingdom* have had a great influence on twentieth-century sacred music and are performed around the world today.

Although *The Dream of Gerontius* is more accessible and therefore more popular, the two oratorios of his New Testament trilogy exemplify the faith of Elgar. In his penetrating book, *The Significance of Elgar*, Jose Everard writes, "It is impossible to fully enter into and understand either the earlier or the Elgarian Oratorios without a preceding familiarity with the New Testament itself, and a faith in and sympathy with the truths and forces therein contained. The Elgarian pair are a veritable musical translation of the Gospel content itself, brought out in a deeply set, contemplative potency, wherein every orchestral and vocal strand serves as an integral part of the thought which it conveys."[19]

Throughout the period in which he worked on these oratorios, Elgar's correspondence shows that he took the work and his personal faith quite seriously. Blending his musical motifs with his understanding of theology, he writes such comments as, "God (in the Old Testament) when influencing persons is called the Spirit of God. The Spirit of God is not something less than God, it is God."[20]

Other letters show Elgar's clever sense of humor. An amusing example is his reply to a letter from the conductor Nicholas Kilburn, who had written for some technical information. Elgar chides his musical friend, "Let your Strings divide themselves *as you* suggest and not according to the judgment of Solomon; the latter plan you will find in a book called (popularly) the Bible, unknown to you, but *perhaps* Mrs. K. may be acquent with it: *cheap editions* may be had."[21]

As is the case of other literary Christians, Elgar's library shelves testify to his faith. He owned numerous editions, including some modern translations, of the Bible, as well as prayer books and commentaries on various books of Scripture. His library also contained many books and essays on theology, a translation of the *Hymns of the Early Church* by J. Brownlie, and a number of works on the history of the early church.[22]

A particular quote of Jean Paul Richter impressed him so much that he always carried it with him: "When in your last hour (think of this) all faculty in the broken spirit shall fade away and die into inanity—imagination, thought, effort, enjoyment—then at last will the night flower of Belief alone continue blooming, and refresh with its perfumes in the last darkness."[23]

Elgar's life and music went through various phases, but he remained a lifelong Christian, even affirming his faith in his last illness and on his deathbed.[24] His reputation as a composer and as a great man would soon spread throughout the musical world. The great pianist Paderewski (who later became the Prime Minister of Poland) was once asked at a party: "Who is Elgar and where did he study? Was he at any conservatory?" When the pianist answered in the negative, he was further questioned: "But who was his teacher?" Paderewski replied quietly, "Le Bon Dieu."[25]

Some Thoughts on Elgar: Loyalty

As one considers the life of Sir Edward Elgar, one can easily find many admirable qualities worthy of emulation: self-control, steadiness, grace, and dignity. Many of these traits he inherited from the refinement of the Edwardian Age as well as from the lineage of his own family. But far and above these social graces, Elgar uniformly displayed an exceptionally deep loyalty to those around him. This devoted allegiance is perhaps best seen in his relationships to his beloved country, to his many friends, and especially to his wife, Lady Alice.

Elgar had a profound love for his country and felt no shame to be a composer in a land that had not produced a major composer for centuries. He dedicated many of his works to members of the royal family, and the honors he received from his king were of great value to him. Since he was too old to be a soldier in World War I, he insisted on joining the volunteer reserve, becoming a military constable, and writing martial music. Rather than apologizing for such popular work for his people, he maintained, "I like to look on the composer's vocation as the old troubadours or bards did. In those days it was no disgrace for a man to be turned on to step in front of an army and inspire them with a song."

To his many friends, his constancy was marked by encouragement and liberal generosity. The many movements of the "Enigma" Variations are each compliments to his closest companions, many of whom were lifelong colleagues. Several of Elgar's musical friends felt the freedom to give him suggestions concerning his compositions when they were first performed. Rather than resent such criticisms, he would patiently listen to his associates and often incorporate their ideas with unfeigned gratitude for their friendship.

Elgar's loyalty to his wife was absolute. In Alice he found not only his wife but his best friend, mentor, supporter, manager, fan, and musical assistant. Of their many friends, not one has reported the least hint of unfaithfulness or even an argument in their long marriage. When she died at the age of seventy-one, her grief-stricken husband placed in her casket the beautiful Court Sword which had been royally bestowed upon him. He gave her credit for all his work, writing after her death to one of his admirers, "You, who like some of my work, must thank *her* for all of it—not me."

Recommended Listening

Orchestral Music: 2 symphonies; the "Enigma" Variations; *Violin Concerto in B Minor; Cello Concerto in E Minor; Salut d'Amour;* "Pomp and Circumstances" marches

Choral Music: *The Dream of Gerontius; Lux Christ; The Apostles; The Kingdom; Scenes from the Saga of King Olaf*

Chamber Music: *String Quartet in E Minor; String Quintet in A Minor*

Songs: *Chariots of the Lord; The Torch; The River; A Child Asleep; The Kingsway*

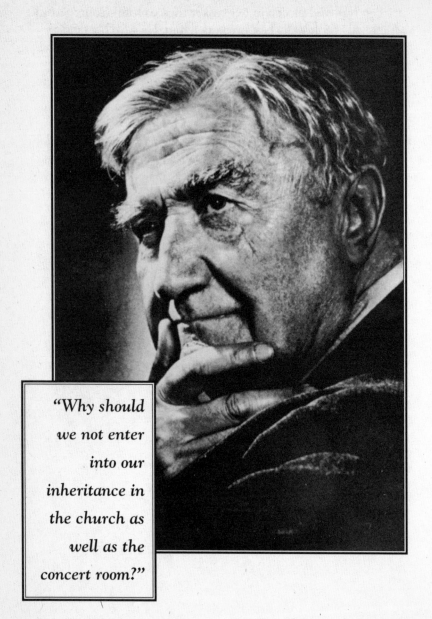

"Why should we not enter into our inheritance in the church as well as the concert room?"

Ralph Vaughan
WILLIAMS

1872–1958

Swimming in the North Sea off the coast of England was usually challenging, but he had always been a fine swimmer. Yet today's waves were overwhelming. Before he knew it, he was being swept farther and farther away from the deserted shore.

What were his thoughts as he battled the surf, struggled for his life? Did he ponder the ridiculous notion that had landed him in this deadly predicament? For he knew that the only reason he had been swimming so much recently was to find inspiration for the composing of a great symphony about the ocean.

Or did he pray to God in those anxious moments, crying out to his Lord for a miraculous rescue? His thoughts were never recorded, but just before he gave himself up for lost a huge wave hurled him onto the rocky shore. Utterly exhausted, he crawled away from the water and lay still for a long time—panting, coughing, thanking God for sparing his life.

The English composer Ralph Vaughan Williams never forgot the inexorable power of the water that almost claimed him. As he had planned, he soon used this memory for tremendous inspiration. The opening of his magnificent *Symphony no. 1* ("A Sea Symphony"), when the chorus sings at full volume, "Behold the sea itself!" is one of the most spectacular moments in the history of music.

From the day of his birth, October 12, 1872, Ralph Vaughan Williams was rooted in the soil of the British countryside. His music would exhibit the national spirit found by Edward Elgar, and extend it into the vast wealth of English folksong. Long after he was internationally known as one of his country's greatest composers, he wrote, "If the roots of your art are firmly planted in your own soil and that soil has anything individually to give you, you may still gain the whole world and not lose your own soul."

His family tree was deep into English and Welsh history. Only a few years before his birth the family was rocked by a great controversy, generated by his great-uncle, none other than the scientist Charles Darwin. His book, *The Origin of Species*, was still hotly debated when, as a young boy, Ralph asked his mother what the tumult was all about. Her common sense brought the controversy down to a child's level of understanding: "The Bible says that God made the world in six days, Great Uncle Charles thinks it took longer: but we need not worry about it, for it is equally wonderful either way."[1] This seemed to satisfy the youth, and he never forgot his mother's answer.

Ralph (who always pronounced his name "Raaf") loved music from an early age, but his quiet personality belied the talent that would one day make him famous. He was neither a prodigy like Mozart nor a late-bloomer like Wagner. Instead, he steadily played music through the years and became a thoroughly rounded musician, with proficiency for musicology, teaching, performing, and lastly composing. He was well into his thirties before he composed anything of great significence.

Before that time, he had received his doctorate in music from Cambridge University and became the organist at London's Saint Barnabas Church. He was soon immersed in the world of choral music, conducted a number of choirs, and helped to organize a local choral society. This gave him valuable experience that would one day reap a harvest in his superb choral compositions.

He was rapidly becoming an expert on church music, giving lectures on this and other musical subjects. He particularly objected to "the false sentimentality of many of our modern hymns as compared to the true feeling and dignity of earler examples."[2] In 1904, he was made the editor of the *English Hymnbook*,[3] which sold over five million copies in the next fifty years. This actually contains some of Vaughan Williams's earliest known melodies, though he insisted on publishing them anonymously. He also edited the popular, *Songs of Praise* in 1925, which contained his songs *Saviour, Again to Thy Dear Name We Raise*, and *At the Name of Jesus*.[4]

It was also around this time that he began a lifelong pursuit, that of collecting English folk music from the rural countryside. Often he would spend weeks riding through the country with notebook and pencil, knocking on doors and asking total strangers if they knew any old folk songs. As one might imagine, this method led to many misadventures, but he eventually compiled a great wealth of his country's musical heritage—much of which he would use in his finest compositions.

This contact with British folk song seemed to inspire his own creative powers, and soon he was taking time for serious composing. In 1908 he traveled to France to study with the eminent composer, Maurice Ravel. The following year he produced his first masterpiece, the *Fantasia on a Theme by Thomas Tallis*, for double string orchestra. This beautiful piece, still one of his most popular and performed works, reflects Vaughan Williams' love for his country's musical past—its theme was composed by an English church composer of the sixteenth century.

When World War I broke out, much of England's musical activity ceased. But nothing could stifle Vaughan Williams' new-found creativity. He was once walking above the cliffs of Dover near a movement of British infantry, when a melody occurred to him and he sat to write it down. Suddenly he was arrested by a young officer, who insisted that the composer's manuscript paper contained "maps, information for the enemy." Fortunately, the officer's superior recognized the music for what it was and allowed the bewildered composer to go free.

Shortly thereafter, Williams began his own military service, which lasted throughout the war. His jobs ranged from stretcher bearer to artillery officer to military choir director.

After the war, Vaughan Williams began teaching at the Royal College of Music, and to continue his energetic composing. His powerful symphonies (like Beethoven, Dvořák, Mahler, and Bruckner, he composed nine in all) were making him known thoughout the world's musical circles. But his emphasis was always on his homeland. In 1935, he was awarded England's highest honor for a composer, the Order of Merit.

The combination of his musicality and his spiritual nature made Vaughan Williams a leading expert on interpreting the great Christian composer, J. S. Bach. During the 1920s he directed London's renowned Bach Choir, and in 1947 he founded the Dorking Bach Choir, into which he poured vast stores of energy until his retirement in 1954. It is from these years that we have the most vivid recollections from his co-workers of the lovable disposition of the master: "Once during a rehearsal of Bach's *Mass in B Minor*, he told us that to sing Bach one needed the "mind of a poet, the heart of a saint and the lungs of a giant!"[5]

His performance of Bach's *St. Matthew Passion* revealed his own spiritual life: "Who among us would ever forget how, at the performance tears would run down his cheeks as the narrator sang of Peter's denial and of the Crucifixion? I remember particularly the intensity he would put into the moment when Judas says '*Master, is it I?*' and Jesus replies, '*Thou hast said*'; he called it, 'one of the saddest moments in the whole of music.'"[6]

"In the *St. Matthew Passion*, at 'Be near me, Lord, when dying,' he produced the most illuminating remark of all: 'Sing this to yourself.'"[7]

His approach to the sublime music of Bach was reverencial. He speaks of the "Quoniam" movement of the *B Minor Mass*—which expresses the words, "Thou only art most high in the glory of God the Father"—as the greatest musical movement ever written.[8] He describes the interpretational principles by quoting Scripture: "'The letter killeth, but the Spirit giveth life.' If we adhere meticulously and mechanically to the letter of Bach we shall inevitably kill the spirit."[9]

Vaughan Williams continued his composing and his many musical activities well into his eighties. On August 26, 1958, he was planning the recording of his *Symphony no. 9*, which had been finished that year. During the night he died in his sleep, of coronary thrombosis.

This great composer, whose name has always been associated with church music, was somewhat reserved about his personal faith. It was usually considered indecorous if not improper for respectable Englishmen to openly show great piety or devotional fervor. Like Edward Elgar before him, Vaughan Williams would best express his convictions through the expressive scriptural music he faithfully composed.

He was born into a religious family, and his father was the Reverend Arthur Vaughan Williams, Master of Arts of Christchurch, Oxford, Vicar of the parish of Down Ampney.[10] Vaughan had been taught the Scriptures from the earliest age, and his Bible—in particular the King James version—remained as one of his essential companions through life.[11] Throughout his long life, he reverently quoted Scripture in his writing and teaching in order to make his points clear.[12]

Vaughan Williams had an ongoing mission to improve the music of the church. He deplored the poor compositional quality in many of his church's hymns and anthems, and he admonished church musicians to not settle for mediocrity. In his exhortations, he noted with dismay that the church often accepted inferior efforts that would have never been tolerated in the secular music world: "Why should we not enter into our inheritance in the church as well as the concert room?"[13]

As one might imagine, this determination for excellence did not always win him friends. Once, he was attacked for his acceptance of liturgical dance. In wrote in defense, "I had hoped that the killjoy and lugubrious view of religion which once obtained was now happily dead, but I fear there are still some people who have a degraded view of the dance and connect it only with high kicking and jazz, but the dance in its highest manifestations shares with music, poetry and painting, one of the greatest means of expression of the very highest of human aspirations. The dance has always been connected with religious fervour—that is, orderly and rhythmical movement surcharged with emotion.

"What are the great Church ceremonies but a sublimation of the dance? What about the 150th Psalm, 'Praise Him with the timbrel and dances'? Surely Bunyan's *Pilgrim's Progress* is full of the highest religious fervour and he made Mr. Ready-to-Halt celebrate his deliverance by dancing."[14]

Williams showed his keen knowledge of Scripture when charged with performing music that included a message of human love. He writes that "Human love has always been taken as a symbol of man's relationship to divine things. *The Song of Solomon* has been treated in all the churches as a symbol of the relationship of God to man. And what about Isaiah and his 'beloved's vineyard'? And is not the Church in the Book of Revelation always symbolized as the bride?"[15]

In his own musical writings, he speaks of the importance of the church's need for music to enhance corporate worship: "Music has always been part of ceremony, especially religious ceremony. From primitive times both song and dance have been part of religious ritual, which calls forth the desire for music, and especially song, to enhance the excitement and spiritual exaltation of the worshippers."[16]

Vaughan Williams' greatest spiritual legacy is found, of course, in his own compositions. The three large works that immediately come to mind—and that biographer Alan Edgar Frederic Dickinson collectively called Vaughan Williams' "affirmations of belief"[17]—are his opera *The Pilgrim's Progress*, the Christmas cantata named *Hodie* ("this day"), and the orchestral suite, *Job—A Masque for Dancing*. All are masterpieces of Christian expression and for the latter work the composer read and reread the book of Job so much that the rhythm of the King James Bible is actually found within the music itself.[18]

Another notable work that imparts Vaughan Williams' faith is his *Five Mystical Songs*, for baritone, chorus, and orchestra.[19] For the texts, he selected poetry by George Herbert, one of England's greatest Christian poets. The manner in which the composer renders the moving poem, "Love" is clearly the work of a master of expression. Herbert's words, "'Know you not,' says love, 'Who bore the blame?'" seem to come directly from the Savior to the heart of every audience.

Other major sacred works include his *Te Deum*, composed for the installation of the Archbishop of Canterbury[20] and the exquisite *Mass in G Minor*. This last piece is considered by many to be Vaughan Williams' greatest sacred opus.[21] As he always attempted to wed his modern compositonal style to that of his country's musical heritage, he must have been gratified by the praise given him by Sir Richard Terry, who had commissioned the work. The composer was assured that "In your individual and modern idiom you have really captured the old liturgical spirit and atmosphere."[22]

But thousands of Christians today know Vaughan Williams through the inspiration of singing his many smaller works, such as *O Taste and See*, *Dona Nobis Pacem*, *O Clap Your Hands*, and his famous arrangement of *Old Hundredth*. Many such pieces were commissioned for specific ocassions, like *The Souls of the Righteous*, a motet that was composed for the Dedication Service of the Battle of Britain Chapel in Westminster Abbey in 1947.[23] But others were composed for the sheer joy they brought the composer; an excellent example of this is his novel arrangement of *The First Nowell*, for chorus and orchestra.[24]

Throughout his life, Ralph Vaughan Williams was a great encouragement to those aaround him, especially the many church musicians he inspired. Musicologist Michael Hurd states that, "As a man Vaughan Williams left an almost universally favorable impression."[25] A critic once said of him that "He sees Heaven open as the door of his own home."[26]

Roy Douglas, a musician who worked on many projects with Vaughan Williams, possesses an unfinished musical score on which the composer was writing just before his death. He notes that "On page 41 he had reached the words 'And by the light of that same star Three Wise Men came from . . .' One turns the page. There are the names of the instruments in the left-hand margin, and nothing else." Then, exhibiting the profound love that all of Vaughan Williams' friends had for him, Douglas writes, "I still find myself deeply moved when I look at this empty page."[27]

Some Thoughts on Vaughan Williams: Simplicity

Perhaps the reason Ralph Vaughan Williams was so attracted to the simplicity of English folk songs is found in the composer's own inherent unpretentiousness. He was never one to put on airs, even after he achieved international fame and was the toast of royalty and high society. Vaughan Williams' personality was unchanged by either his circumstances or the company of dissimilar people. His many friends always knew where they stood with him, and their affection for him was enhanced by his native simplicity of character.

It is interesting to hear observations about this world-famous composer. Even those who dearly loved him were often amused by his unsophisticated demeanor. A musician who knew him, once remarked, "Vaughan Williams looks like a farmer on his way to judge the shorthorns at an agricultural fair." The American composer Aaron Copland once said, "His is the music of a gentleman-farmer." Many of his compositions, particularly his beautiful *Symphony no. 3* ("Pastoral Symphony"), bring forth a simple, rural ambience.

His genuine simplicity made him respect all people, regardless of their rank in British society. Vaughan Williams never let his fame distance him from the average Englishman. Once he walked into a chorus rehearsal where his *Symphony no. 1* ("Sea Symphony") was being prepared. Before the group realized he was there, the master slipped into the bass section, where he mumbled to one of its astonished singers, "I'd better sit next to you as I don't know this myself!"

Perhaps the best picture of Vaughan Williams' childlike disposition is found in a letter he wrote to a nine-year-old boy. Apparently the youth had attended a concert that included a Haydn symphony as well as the *Symphony no. 8* of Vaughan Williams. Afterward this boy wrote a letter to the conductor, Sir John Barbirolli, expressing how much he liked the Haydn symphony but not the other one. Barbirolli gave the composer this letter, which so delighted Vaughan Williams that he immediately wrote the boy:

Dear Tom,

Sir John Barbirolli has sent me your letter to him—I am glad you like Haydn. He was a very great man and wrote beautiful tunes. I must one day try to write a tune which you will like.

Yours affectionately,
R. V. Williams

Recommended Listening

Orchestral Music: 9 symphonies, notably his "Sea" Symphony (no. 1), "London" Symphony (no. 2), "Pastoral" Symphony (no. 3), and "Sinfonia Antartica" (no. 7); *Job—A Masque for Dancing; Fantasia on a Theme by Thomas Tallis; Concerto for Oboe; Concerto for Tuba; Concerto for Violin*

Choral Music: *O Taste and See; Dona Nobis Pacem; O Clap your Hands; Old Hundredth; The Souls of the Righteous; Te Deum; Mass in G Minor*

Cantatas: *Hodie; The Sons of Light; Dona Nobis Pacem*

Opera: *Pilgrim's Progress; Sir John in Love*

Chamber Music: *Sonata for Violin and Piano; Quartet in A Minor; Quartet in G Minor*

Songs: *Five Mystical Songs; Songs of Travel*

"Most of the
forward movements
of life in general
. . . have been the
work of essentially
religious-minded
men."

Charles
IVES

1874–1954

A *passerby listening to the jarring song and accompaniment coming from the Connecticut house would never have believed a music lesson was in progress. More likely, the odd-sounding noise would be chalked up to the antics of preteen boys mocking a matronly piano teacher. Yet a lesson is exactly what is happening.*

The father, an innovative bandmaster, sits at the piano, methodically playing Stephen Foster's "Swannee River" in the key of C. His ten-year-old son struggles to keep up with the accompaniment as he sings the lyrics. The boy finds he is up against a difficult challenge: His father insists that he sing in the key of E-flat.

The young boy grimaces in concentration. Producing the correct vocal line to this accompaniment takes not only vocal control but an advanced understanding of music theory. "Again!" cries the father. Finally, the father calls a halt to his outrageous venture. The boy's relief is profound, yet the clashing sounds linger in his memory and ignite a lifelong curiosity about breaching the boundaries of traditional music.

The boy's father, meanwhile, is delighted with his son's progress. He proclaims, "Now that kind of exercise will really help you to stretch your ears." Based on the compositions Charles Ives would eventually create, it seems these experimental lessons worked.

Charles Ives, a wonderful and notorious composer from the United States, appears to be several men rolled into one. The New Englander excelled in many areas, becoming a composer, a successful insurance executive, an excellent athlete, a political idealist, an Emersonian visionary, and a hymn-singing advocate for "that old-time religion."[1] Even his friends had a hard time agreeing on who he was: their descriptions range from lauding Ives as a humble, shy lover of humankind,[2] to censuring him as an opinionated, crotchety old man who could explode at a moment's notice.[3]

Ives was born in Danbury, Connecticut, on October 20, 1874. His father, George Ives, was a gifted musician but a very unconventional music teacher.[4] Later in life, when asked about his musical training, Charles Ives would simply reply, "Pa taught me what I know." He also remembered, "Father thought that a man as a rule did not use the facilities that the Creator had given hard enough."[5] So the bandmaster persisted in subjecting his talented son to a wide variety of experimental musical concepts. It is no surprise that the name Charles Ives eventually became synonymous with outlandish dissonance, polytonality (he said he liked to "hog all the keys"), and even the beginnings of what is now called aleatory or "chance" music.

Today there are Charles Ives Music Festivals, scholarly editions of his works, books, articles, and even a Charles Ives Society. Yet this widely celebrated man remained virtually unknown until he stopped writing music about 1925.[6] He was quite shy about his compositions and never tried to force his music on the public. Often, years would go by before he heard his works performed, and many more years passed before their genius was understood and appreciated. His *Third Symphony* was not played until thirty-five years after it was written. When it finally emerged from obscurity, it won the Pulitzer Prize for Music.

Ives' music tested the limits of conventional composition and introduced many unexpected and novel elements. A typical work is his complex *Second String Quartet*, subtitled "String Quartet for four men—who converse, discuss, argue, fight, shake hands, shut up—then walk to the mountainside to view the firmament." In another work, entitled *All the Way Around and Back*, Ives included this handwritten notation: "foul ball—and the base runner on 3rd has to go all the way back to 1st."

As a young man, Ives enrolled in Yale to study music, but he dumbfounded his teachers, maintaining a consistent D+ average. This was primarily because he spent so much time excelling at baseball, football, and track. One of his coaches declared it a "crying shame" that such a natural athlete wasted so much time in music.[7]

After graduating, Ives abandoned music as a career, believing his unconventional compositions would never attract the popular following needed to make a living. Instead, he entered the insurance business, insisting that he did not want his family to "starve on my dissonances." He eventually cofounded a flourishing insurance company, known as Ives and Myrick. In this field he was also a pioneer, developing the first training course for representatives and formulating the concept of estate planning. The firm prospered and became one of the largest of its kind in the country.[8]

At night and on weekends, Ives shed his businessman's demeanor and immersed himself in composing. Late into the night he experimented on the piano, creating vast quantities of his ultra-complex music. His neighbors frequently objected to the din, complaining that he created "resident disturbances."[9]

Ives' faith and his musical genius are inseparable. Even as a boy, he played the organ for many different churches,[10] giving him a lifelong affinity for sacred choral music.[11] He set to music numerous psalms,[12] and he borrowed extensively from gospel hymn tunes, often highlighting them in the most unusual musical circumstances. From his orchestral compositions to his multifarious chamber music, more than fifty different hymn tunes are "quoted,"[13] such as "Aberystwyth" ("Jesus, Lover of My Soul"), "Woodworth" ("Just As I Am Without One Plea"), and "Converse" ("What a Friend We Have in Jesus").[14] His complete works contain dozens of religious titles and references, from *The Revival Service* to *General William Booth Enters into Heaven*.[15]

Ives frequented the outdoor revivals of his time, and their rugged, homespun music affected him deeply.[16] He perceived an authentic, if roughhewn, faith at work among the people who turned out to hear itinerant preachers and evangelists. In his typical, rugged manner, Ives considered these revivals, "a man's experience for men."[17] And hearing them sing brought Ives in touch with the raw persuasion of music. "There was power and exaltation in these great concaves of sound,"[18] he wrote, "sung by thousands of 'let out' souls," as he called them.[19] Sometimes he accompanied the singing himself on the melodeon (a small reed organ),[20] and he listened closely, intrigued, as the fervor of the singing would often throw the key as much as a whole tone higher. His father, who usually led the outdoor congregations with his cornet,[21] had a special sliding valve added so he could rise with the singers and not keep them down![22]

Ives brought the same sort of eclectic mix of influences to his religious faith that he applied to his music, and perhaps that is why his strong faith has been largely misunderstood. It is a curious combination of seemingly opposing forces: On one hand, it is rooted in the "uncivilized" Holy Ghost revivals and open-air preaching he loved,[23] and which many secular biographers fail to understand or appreciate. On the other hand, Ives found personal inspiration in the writings of the great American transcendentalists, notably Emerson and Thoreau.[24] These meditations, in turn, are rarely understood or appreciated by revivalists and fundamentalist Christians.

But Ives saw no contradiction. He lived simultaneously in both worlds and developed a truly unique Christian faith: a childlike yet masculine trust in God, inseparably linked with intellectual integrity. If the transcendentalists and "the prayer-meeting evangelists disagreed on doctrine," wrote one of Ives' biographers, "it seems neither to have upset him or even to have occurred to him."[25]

People close to the composer knew him as deeply religious[26] and very strict on matters of morality.[27] Ives did not bow to intellectual pressure to disparage religious faith. He observed, "Most of the forward movements of life in general and of pioneers in most of the great activities, have been the work of essentially religious-minded men."[28] He openly looked forward to life after death, noting that he wanted to "see and talk to my father."[29]

Ives enjoyed a long and happy marriage to Harmony Twichell, a daughter of a prominent Hartford minister. She was known as a devout woman, who regularly read the Bible aloud to her husband.[30] Despite his Protestant background, Ives maintained an open-minded outlook on the different views of various denominations.[31] Robert M. Crunden, who lectured on the composer's beliefs at the Charles Ives Centennial Festival in 1974, said, "Ives's religion was definitely Christian, but he had no illusions about the stuffiness of churches on many occasions."[32] Ives once observed that "every thinking man knows that the church part of the church always has been dead—that part seen by candle-light, not Christ-light."[33]

Many present-day devotees of Ives' music tend to emphasize the transcendental influence present in his life and work. Perhaps this is a reflection of their own sense of distance from "hell-fire evangelists" and emotional revival meetings. But his principal biographer, John Kirkpatrick, who knew Ives better than anyone living today, wrote: "His church-going self was conservative to the point of fundamentalism. He was almost in a state of 'Give me that old-time religion, it's good enough for me.'"[34]

Some Thoughts on Ives: Unselfishness

In an era when composers often stand accused of lusting after fame, money, or both, it is refreshing to discover a man such as Charles Ives. He knew that both fame and wealth were within his grasp, and he chose neither. Perhaps he saw the folly of chasing such fantasies, or perhaps he simply had better things to do.

Ives' prosperous insurance company could have made him a millionaire many times over, but he insisted on being paid only what would befit his family's needs. He also refused to accept money derived from his musical genius. When he won the coveted Pulitzer Prize in 1947, he told the award committee, "Prizes are for boys. I'm grown up." Ives gave away the $500 prize money.

At first, he actually objected to copyrighting his compositions, firmly believing that everyone should have free access to his work. Finally he did submit to the usual copyright procedures but only on the condition that any profits his music earned would go toward aiding the publication of young composers. His personal generosity toward fellow musicians is legendary.

As to fame, Ives all but hid from it. In his later years, when he began to be proclaimed a genius, he became conspicuously absent from performances of his own work. The composer's nephew, who knew him well, remembers an approachable, unpretentious man: "I never had any compunction about violating the privacy of Uncle Charlie's music studio. In fact, Uncle Charlie never called it a studio. That would have been too fancy a term. It was just a room where the piano was."

This simplicity did not arise out of insecurity or self-doubt. On the contrary, he privately made it clear that he thought his compositions were greater than Mozart's: "I state that it is better! Ask any good musician—those who don't agree with me are not good musicians." But he steadfastly refused to be taken in by worldly trappings. His secretary once asked Ives for an autograph to give her son, and he replied, "The only time you get my autograph is on a check."

Ives reserved a particular fondness for everyday people. "He was always interested in the underprivileged and physically handicapped," his nephew recalled. "He had a sincere interest in anyone who needed help." Although he could explode with rage over such issues as war and politics, he extended kindness to the humblest acquaintance. A widow who worked as the Ives' housekeeper for seventeen years cherishes distinct memories of the famous composer: Ives regularly made friendly jokes, insisted on helping with the dishes, and played hymns on the piano, she recalled.

Such unguarded moments of the man round out a portrait of Charles Ives. He was not just the revolutionary innovator but also a generous, down-to-earth man who loved God and people. His fame was late in coming, but his ultimate influence on other composers has been extraordinary. His famous fellow composer Igor

Stravinsky concluded, "Ives was an original man, a gifted man, a courageous man. Let us honor him through his works."

Recommended Listening

Orchestral Music: 4 symphonies, *Lincoln, the Great Commoner, The Unanswered Question, Robert Browning Overture*
Chamber Music: 2 string quartets
Vocal Music: *General William Booth Enters into Heaven; Psalm 24; Psalm 54; Psalm 67; Psalm 90*
Piano Music: second piano sonata (*Concord, Mass., 1840–60*)

"The more one separates oneself from the canons of the Christian church, the further one distances oneself from the truth."

Igor
STRAVINSKY

1882–1971

It is 1913, and a ballet performance in Paris is agitating its audience into extreme pandemonium. Greeting the ballet's first notes from a solo bassoon are rancorous catcalls from parts of the audience. Others bellow back, defending the peculiar music and dance on the stage. Soon the orchestra is all but drowned out by the riotous din, but still the musicians and dancers persevere.

The music's rhythmic power so overcomes one man in the audience that he begins beating his fists on the head of the man sitting in front of him. In the aisles, tuxedo-clad Frenchmen punch each other like ruffians. The Austrian Ambassador laughs aloud in scorn; a princess storms out of the theater, fuming that she's been made a fool of; and a duel is arranged between two strangers who disagree about the music.

Famous musicians in the audience react with similar passions. In the middle of the maelstrom, Saint-Saens is heard repeating over and over "He is crazy, he is crazy!" Capu screams that the music is a huge fraud, but Ravel shouts "Genius!" Roland-Manuel boldly defends the music and gets his collar torn from his shirt, while Debussy pleads futilely with everyone to quiet down so he can hear. Backstage, trying valiantly to hold back more fights, stands the diminutive composer. The premiere of his Rite of Spring becomes a turning point in Western art, and Igor Stravinsky emerges as the musical master of his century.

There was practically no genre of music beyond the command of Igor Stravinsky, widely considered the most important composer of the twentieth century. He wrote ballet and chamber music, opera, choral, and orchestral music, and that's not all. He composed a polka for Ringling Brothers/Barnum & Bailey Circus and a clarinet concerto for Benny Goodman.

Born in a suburb of St. Petersburg, Russia, Stravinsky received scant encouragement to follow in the musical footsteps of his father, a successful opera singer. Like several composers before him, Stravinsky found himself steered firmly toward the study of law—a more stable and secure way to make a living, so his father believed. Stravinsky obliged his parents, but he continued to compose music whenever he could. Eventually, his devotion to music prevailed and he abandoned his legal studies.

In his early twenties, Stravinsky became the private student of Russian composer Rimsky-Korsakoff. Soon, his genius came to be recognized by the musical world. He gained international attention with the premieres of three great ballets, commissioned by Diaghilev, the renowned director of the Russian Ballet. These works, *Firebird*; *Petrushka*; and the indomitable *Rite of Spring*, subtitled "Pictures of Pagan Russia," remain in the repertoire of every major orchestra in the world today.

Stravinsky's early ballets explore secular and even pagan subjects that offer no clue as to the personal religious faith he possessed later in life. These great works were written when Stravinsky was in his thirties and had long since abandoned the Russian Orthodox faith of his upbringing.[1] Yet in the mid 1920s, Stravinsky experienced a permanent conversion to Christianity.[2]

In the church of his childhood, Stravinsky had been required to read the Bible.[3] He began criticizing and rebelling against the church when he reached his teens,[4] and he parted ways with orthodoxy for nearly three decades. Yet late in life he would explain, "For some years before my conversion, a mood of acceptance had been cultivated in me by a reading of the Gospels and by other religious literature."[5]

Two incidents appeared to assure his newfound faith in Christ. One was an immediate and convincing answer to a private prayer,[6] and the other was a healing experience. Stravinsky developed a painful abscess on his right forefinger, and its insistent throbbing threatened to keep him from performing his *Piano Sonata*. He prayed about the problem but fully expected the concert would have to be canceled.

The pain hounded him all the way to the stage. Later he explained to his friend Robert Craft: "My finger was still festering when I walked onto the stage at the Teatro La Fevice, and I addressed the audience, apologizing in advance for what would have to be a poor performance. I sat down, removed the little bandage, felt the pain had suddenly stopped, and discovered that the finger was—miraculously, it seemed to me—healed."[7]

Soon, Stravinsky began to speak openly of his convictions. In an interview in Brussels, the composer stated, "The more one separates oneself from the canons of the Christian church, the further one distances oneself from the truth.... Art is made of itself, and one cannot create upon a creation, even though we are ourselves graftings of Jesus Christ."[8]

He dedicated his next major composition, the *Symphony of Psalms*, to the glory of God.[9] Like so many of the biblical passages this work contains, the *Symphony of Psalms* expresses an awakening sense of distance from the Creator, and the human choice to return to the Creator. "The first movement was written in a state of religious and musical ebullience," Stravinsky explained. The second movement, Psalm 40, "is a prayer that the new canticle may be put into our mouths. The *Alleluia* [third movement] is that canticle."[10]

Francis Routh, one of Stravinsky's biographers, insisted, "No composer could write such a work without a very secure, rock-like, religious faith."[11] Another biographer, Alexandre Tansman, wrote, "He is a believer in the full sense of the term."[12] Stravinsky's colleague and principal biographer Robert Craft agrees. He has written, "Having lived for more than a quarter of a century with

Stravinsky, and much of that under the same roof, I knew him to be, as the saying goes, profoundly religious."[13]

The composer had strong opinions about the purpose and use of music. "The church knew what the psalmist knew: Music praises God. Music is as well or better able to praise Him than the building of the church and all its decorations; it is the church's greatest ornament."[14] When asked if one must be a believer to compose church music, Stravinsky asserted, "Certainly, and not merely a believer in 'symbolic figures,' but in the person of the Lord, the person of the Devil, and the miracles of the church."[15]

Stravinsky had his quirks, and some of them found expression in the way he integrated faith into his life. He grumbled about the "you who's" in new translations of the Bible,[16] and he always prayed in the Slavonic language of the Russian liturgy.[17] Other eccentricities were innocuous and endearing. Stravinsky often balanced an extra pair of glasses on top of his head in case he lost the pair he was wearing!

Once his biographer Craft accompanied the composer to his Orthodox Church. As soon as he entered, Stravinsky prostrated himself flat on the floor before the altar and prayed. For two hours, the two men knelt on a hard, uncushioned floor. After taking the sacraments, Stravinsky again prayed with his head touching the floor.[18]

The composer certainly loved his church, yet he retained a sense of honest detachment from it. He wrote *Three Sacred Choruses* to be used in its liturgy,[19] stating that the work was "inspired by the bad music and worse singing in the Russian Church."[20] Harboring no sectarian prejudice, he also wrote a Catholic Mass which, he believed, "appeals directly to the spirit."[21] Other works based on sacred texts include *The Flood*, *The Tower of Babel*, *Abraham and Isaac*, *Requiem Canticles*, *Sermon*, a *Narrative* and a *Prayer*, *Threni*, *Canticum Sacrum*, a *Credo*, an *Ave Maria*, and a *Pater Noster*.

In his work, Stravinsky found expression for his views on Christianity. In his working notes to *The Flood*, for instance, he described Noah "as an Old Testament Christ-figure, like

Melchizedek."[22] He seemed especially preoccupied with the nature of evil, writing, "As Satan's falsetto aria with flutes is a prolepsis of Christianity, Satan must now be shown as Anti-Christ."[23] He went on to make a thought-provoking theological observation, noting that Lucifer is "inclined to take his position for granted, which is why true Christians can overcome him."[24]

Throughout his life, Stravinsky was known for his integrity and candor. Concerning his genius, he wrote, "I regard my talents as God-given, and I have always prayed to Him for strength to use them. When in early childhood I discovered that I had been made the custodian of musical aptitudes, I pledged myself to God to be worthy of their development, though, of course, I have broken the pledge and received uncovenanted mercies all my life, and though the custodian has all too often kept faith on his all-too-worldly terms."[25]

Stravinsky faced up to his own imperfections without flinching. In his personal writings entitled "Thoughts of an Octogenarian," he observed, "I was born out of time in the sense that by temperament and talent I would have been more suited for the life of a small Bach, living in anonymity and composing regularly for an established service and for God. I did weather the world I was born to, weathered it well, you will say, and I have survived—though not uncorrupted."[26]

Once he replied to what he considered an unfair criticism of the vocal writing of his sacred music, commenting dryly, "One hopes to worship God with a little art if one has any, and if one hasn't, and cannot recognize it in others, then one can at least burn a little incense."[27] Concerning the origin of his innovative compositions, he was almost blunt in his modesty: "Only God can create. I make music from music."[28]

Stravinsky lived a full, long life enriched by a wide circle of friends, all of whom respected his Christian beliefs. As he concluded in his acclaimed "Poetics of Music," he believed "Music comes to reveal itself as a form of communion with our fellow man—and with the Supreme Being."[29]

Some Thoughts on Stravinsky: Integrity

Stravinsky's many years as a composer were lived in the public eye. His life and his work have endured more scrutiny than any serious composer of this century. Yet the more one studies this man, the more he appears as a Gibraltar who remained unshaken by the opinions and pressures of the world around him. To maintain his personal integrity, he spent decades "going against the grain." He managed to preserve a basic consistency that was rarely seen in the lives of his artistic colleagues.

To begin with, Stravinsky was a musical pathfinder, establishing bold new concepts yet remaining unruffled by the often venomous criticism his innovations provoked. He was not an imitator; he followed his own lead, single-handedly creating whole schools of musical thought. After stretching the bounds of complexity in his early ballets, he championed neoclassicism, and later even tried his hand at serial compositions. Yet none of these moves came about because of exterior pressures or intimidation. Stravinsky leaves the impression that if he ever used a device that was common among other composers, it was due to coincidence rather than imitation.

His spiritual life reflected his moral integrity. When he later came to believe the truth of Christianity, Stravinsky did not hesitate to declare himself openly a convert. He even wrote his famous collaborator, Diaghilev, to explain his new convictions and ask forgiveness for any wrong he may have ever committed against him. He seemed to consider honest acknowledgment to be the only consistent choice before him. His religious beliefs, which might have drawn ridicule from the world, were repeatedly asserted without hesitation or apology.

After his conversion, Stravinsky led a consistent spiritual life and adhered to it without compromise to its standards. Many first-hand evidences of his religious congruity are told with respect by colleagues who did not share his faith. In their presence, the composer worshiped unblushingly, showed displeasure or even irritation at things he considered blasphemous, and spoke openly about his Christian faith and its effect on his life and work.

Stravinsky held deep convictions, and he could be adamant about them. This was not due to a quarrelsome spirit but, rather, to his unconquerable integrity. Yet with all the controversy his music created, he still welcomed an encouraging word. When a friend informed Stravinsky that he was preparing a biography about him, the composer answered, "If you are really writing a book about me, say what you have to say." Then he added with a smile, "But please be kind."

Recommended Listening

Orchestral Music: *Suites from The Firebird, Petrouchka, Rite of Spring, Symphonies of Wind Instruments; Symphony in C Major; Concerto for Violin*

Chamber Music: *The Soldier's Tale; Octet for Winds*

Piano Music: *Sonata for Piano*

Choral Music: *Symphony of Psalms; Pater Noster; Mass*

Opera: *The Nightingale; The Flood*

"I'm a composer
because I
love music and
a Christian
because I
believe."

Olivier
MESSIAEN

1908–1992

The prisoners awoke to another cold, dismal day in their prison camp, Stalag 8A in Silesia. It was January 15, 1941, but most of these ragged, underfed men had long since forgotten such niceties as calendars and dates. Ever since Germany had overrun France, these prisoners had nothing to expect but starvation, mistreatment, and death.

Yet today was to be different from their wretched routine. Their captors had given permission for several of the prisoners to give a concert. Desperate for a taste of culture, or anything to remind them of better times, 5000 of these pathetic men surged toward the makeshift stage.

There sat several of their own: a cellist who held a battered instrument having only three strings, also a clarinetist and a violinist. Next to them stood a dilapidated upright piano—they would soon hear that it was horribly out of tune and many of its keys were broken.

As the pianist entered, it was announced that he was also the composer of the new piece the little group would perform. It had been composed in the prison camp, and bore the apocalyptic title Quartet for the End of Time. For many in the audience, this would be the last music they would ever hear. Fortunately, its composer, Olivier Messiaen, would be repatriated the following year. But he never forgot that performance and would often assert

that his music had never been listened to with such attention and
understanding than on that cold day in Stalag 8A.

It is appropriate to end this book with a composer such as Olivier Messiaen. He was not only one of France's greatest musicians, but was one of the most outspoken Christian composers of all time. Rather than sifting through hundreds of letters to find references to belief, we have our choice of dozens of complete and detailed accounts of Messiaen's devout faith in Christ.

His music is so innovative and complex that much of it still awaits its fullest appreciation. Many times in his career Messiaen's music was spurned by both believers and unbelievers. The former because of their unfamiliarity with the challenges of contemporary music, the latter because of their unfamiliarity with the sacred truths Messiaen was attempting to convey. Yet by the end of his long life, both the composer and his many compositions had won universal recognition and praise.

He was born on December 10, 1908, in Avignon. Messiaen's parents were devout Catholics, and his creative gifts were greatly encouraged by their love of artistry and culture—his father was a Shakespearian scholar and his mother a poet. At the age of nine he wrote his first composition (*The Lady of Shalott*, for piano solo) and in 1919 entered the Paris Conservatoire. When he was twenty-two, he was appointed organist of the Church of La Sainte Trinite in Paris, where he would faithfully serve for decades. He remembered, "Every Sunday I've played for three Masses and Vespers, and often funerals and weddings during the week."[1]

Five years later, Messiaen married the violinist Claire Delbos. She inspired him to compose his first song-cycle, *Poemes pour Mi*, which extols the spiritual significance of marriage. When their first son was born, he wrote a song-cycle about parenthood, *Chants de terre at de ciel.*

When World War II engulfed France, he joined the army. He was captured in 1940 by the Germans while trying to escape on an old bicycle. Among his few possessions that accompanied him to

Stalag 8A were scores of Bach's *Brandenburg* concerti, and others by Beethoven, Ravel, Berg, and Stravinsky. During his two-year imprisonment, Messiaen wrote his *Quartet for the End of Time*, which has become one of the twentieth century's greatest pieces of chamber music.

After his repatriation, he was appointed Professor of Harmony at the Paris Conservatoire. For many years, he would have a profound influence on the next generation of musicians, among them Karlheinz Stockhausen and Pierre Boulez. He expected a great deal from his students but also encouraged them to explore their compositional freedom. He once explained this "freedom" as having "nothing to do with fantasy, disorder, revolt or indifference. It is a constructive freedom, which is arrived at through self-control, respect for others, a sense of wonder of that which is created, meditation on the mystery and the search for the Truth. This wonderful freedom is like a foretaste of the freedom of Heaven. Christ promised it to his disciples when he said: 'If you continue in my word, then . . . you will know the truth, and the truth will make you free'" (John 8:32).[2]

A turning point in his compositional career was in 1945 when he premiered his *Trois Petites Liturgies de la Presense Divine*, for women's voices and orchestra. It created a fury of controversy. Its spiritual text was little appreciated by the secular critics, and the Christians in his audience were offended by the dissonant music. But when the storm cleared, Messiaen's reputation was assured, and he spent the rest of his life composing masterpieces—many of which attest to his strong faith.

In 1949, Messiaen was invited to teach in America at the Tanglewood Music Festival. Such renowned musicians as Bernstein and Koussevitsky recognized his genius and championed his music. He began to see his works performed around the globe by the world's finest musicians and ensembles. In 1978 and 1979, Messiaen toured the major cities of America and finished with a "Messiaen Week" of concerts at New York's Lincoln Center to honor his seventieth birthday. When the composer died on April 27, 1992, he was mourned by the entire musical world.

Messiaen's fervent Catholic faith is quite well known. When his biographer Claude Samuel asked, "What impressions do you want to communicate to your listeners?" he replied, "The first idea that I wished to express—and the most important, because it stands above them all—is the existence of the truths of the Catholic faith. I've the good fortune to be a Catholic. I was born a believer, and it happens that the Scriptures struck me even as a child."[3] He insisted, "I'm a composer because I love music, and a Christian because I believe."[4]

Messiaen gave two extended interviews on the subject of his faith to Almut Robler, who then wrote the excellent book, *Contributions to the Spiritual World of Olivier Messiaen*. The author gives a portrait of a man with strong convictions concerning his Savior: "Through Christ, the wonderful knowledge has been bestowed on us that this God, who's beyond Time, to whom nothing out of time or space clings, that He who is completely different from everything and is contained in Himself—that He came in order to suffer with us."[5] At another time, Messiaen states, "The resurrection is the cause and the root of our hope."[6]

He also saw clearly the obstacles that non-Christians faced in their unbelief. In an interview, Messiaen pointed out that "The difficulty for unbelievers is to acknowledge that Christ is God."[7] Concerning the need for faith, he quoted the story of Jesus calling Peter to walk toward him on the water, then he added, "That's how it is for all of us every day. We must constantly strive afresh not to doubt and not to drown. We must direct our gaze towards the life hereafter and try to forget about this life."[8]

Although Messiaen's background was within the Catholic Church, he recognized that God's truth abounded through all of Christianity. He remarked, "I'm a Christian, we're all Christians and I think that in the present age of ecumenism—as, furthermore, in every era—we shouldn't attach too much importance to religious differences."[9] His emphasis was the central point of all Christian faith, Jesus Christ: "He appears to us—came to us and tried to make Himself comprehensible in our language, in our sensations, in our attitudes of mind. That's the most beautiful aspect of the God-head: the Mystery of the Incarnation, and that's why I'm a Christian. In saying this, I'm not thinking about differences between Orthodox Christians, Protestants, Catholics—and a Christian is a person who understands that God came."[10]

Messiaen's music reflects the man himself and his beliefs. Using his talents for the secular concert halls as well as for the church, he claimed, "I wished to accomplish a liturgical act—that is to say, to transfer a kind of divine office, a kind of communal praise to the concert hall."[11] Explaining the great diversity within his musical style, he said, "God for me is manifest, and my conception of sacred music derives from this conviction. God being present in all things, music dealing with theological subjects can and must be extremely varied."[12]

He also had strong opinions about aleatory or "chance" music, which he insisted was due to his theology. "I don't believe in chance because I'm a Christian; I believe in Providence and I think that all that happens is foreseen. Certainly the freedom of events is respected but, for God who sees everything simultaneously, there's no chance."[13]

Messiaen knew that his vision of merging his concert music and his faith would be resisted. Concerning his first major controversy, he notes, "I've imposed the truths of the Faith on the concert room, but in a liturgical sense. Proof of this is that my main religious concert work is called *Trois petites Liturgies*. I didn't choose this title idly: I thought of performing a liturgical act, that is to say, transporting a kind of Office, a kind of organized act of praise into the concert room. This—I repeat—scandalized some people, but my chief originality is to have taken the idea of the Catholic liturgy from the stone buildings intended for religious services and to have installed it in other buildings not intended for this kind of music and which, finally, have received it very well."[14]

Many of his works specifically refer to his Christian faith. His *Couleurs de la Cite celeste* interprets the colors mentioned in the book of Revelation.[15] The organ work, *La Nativite du Seigneur*, focuses on Jesus as the Christ Child as well as the Word of God.[16]

The Quartet for the End of Time is dedicated to the angel in the book of Revelation, "who lifts his hand towards the heaven saying 'There shall be no more time.'"[17] The topic for his opera, *Saint Francois d'Assise* was chosen because Francis is "the saint who most resembles Christ."[18]

Like many Christian composers before him, Messiaen was known to jot expressions of his faith on his musical scores. In the movement, "Desseins eternels" from *La Nativite du Seigneur*, he wrote the Bible verses, "God, in his love, has chosen me to be his adopted son, through Jesus Christ, to the praise and glory of his grace" (Ephesians 1:5–6).[19] Inscribed on the orchestra score of *Le tombeau resplendissant* is a poem by Messiaen which begins, "I sing the gift of the divine essence, The body of Jesus Christ, his body and his blood."[20]

His compositions employed a huge array of musical material, including his church's plainchant, which he called an "inexhaustible mine of rare and expressive melodic contours."[21] His appreciation of nature—and especially birdsong—find their way into many of his works. But he kept his love of nature secondary to his love of God: "Like St. Paul, I see in nature a manifestation of one of the aspects of divinity, but it's equally certain that God's creations are not God himself."[22]

Messiaen studied and incorporated complex rhythms from different cultures throughout the world, particularly Hindu rhythms. This has led some musicians to speculate whether the composer exhibited a propensity toward Eastern religions. But when confronted with this misunderstanding, Messiaen was forthright: "No, no! I have a great admiration for Hindu rhythms, but only for the rhythms, not for Indian philosophy. I've studied it in order to understand the rhythms, but I'm not at all Hindu or Shivaist. As for Buddhism, it's all about a theory of emptiness, of passivity."[23]

One of the aspects of Messiaen's life that endeared him to so many admirers was his peaceful composure and his thoughtfulness of others. Claude Samuel once commented on the composer's facility to rise above the hustle and bustle of the millions in Paris all around him. Messiaen seemed almost disturbed by this aptitude, conceding, "You're probably right and I'm probably in the wrong to be so; as a Christian, I should interest myself in everyone and love my neighbor."[24]

The twenty-first century will confirm whether Messiaen's music will stand the test of time, but already his genius has been universally acclaimed. Yet his personal modesty would never allow him to assume long-term greatness on the basis of his present success. Rather, he advanced the need for dedicated Christian musicians. In an article in which he celebrated sacred music, Messiaen concluded, "To express with a lasting power our darkness struggling with the Holy Spirit, to raise upon the mountain the doors of our prison of flesh, to give to our century the spring water for which it thirsts, there shall have to be a great artist who will be both a great artisan and a great Christian."[25]

For the thousands of us who love both the man and his imaginative music, it would seem that such a great artist is indeed found in the composer Olivier Messiaen.

Some Thoughts on Messiaen: Boldness

Messiaen was a man of faith living in an age and a society almost devoid of faith. Although much of his life was spent in the service of the church, his compositions and illustrious career were spent in the core of the secular music world. The temptation to be silent about his beliefs was ever present, especially when his audience was often only interested in his musical genius. Yet without compromise, he used his compositions, his speeches, his teaching, his writings, and his interviews as a steadfast witness for Christ.

Consider the opening of a typical speech in Amsterdam: "I've been asked to deliver a confession of my faith, that is, to talk about what I believe, what I love, what I hope for. What do I believe? That doesn't take long to say and in it everything is said at once: I believe in God. And because I believe in God, I believe likewise in the Holy Trinity and in the Holy Spirit (to whom I've dedicated my "Messe de la Pentecote"), and in the Son, the Word made Flesh, Jesus Christ (to whom I've dedicated a large part of my works)."

Were people in the audience uncomfortable at this unashamed Christian? If so, it seems not to have bothered Messiaen. He seems to have spoken with the same conviction to music critics as he would have in a conversation with his church. Indeed, his unaffected confidence had the effect of earning his listeners' respect. All of his biographers, including those who did not share Messiaen's faith, express a profound admiration for the uncompromising message of the man and his music.

It is also clear that his boldness is not merely an aspect of his personality but is generated by the sincerity of his faith. Although he knew he possessed musical genius, he still considered his beliefs far more important: "That is the first aspect of my work, the noblest and, doubtless, the most useful and valuable; perhaps the only one which I won't regret at the hour of my death."

The legacy of Olivier Messiaen is more than that of a brilliant composer. He also leaves us an excellent example of modeling the Christian walk in a secular environment. The witness to Christ's love portrayed in his life now lives on in the works which he composed for the glory of God.

Recommended Listening

Orchestra Music: *Chronochromie; Seven Haikai; Colors of the Heavenly City; Turangalila-Symphonie; Et exspecto resurrectionem mortuorum*

Chamber Music: *Quartet for the End of Time*

Choral Music: *The Transfiguration of our Lord Jesus Christ*

Keyboard Music: *Meditations on the Mystery of the Sacred Trinity* (for organ); *Catalogue of Birds* (for piano)

Afterword

The study of great composers' lives should be more than academic exercise. Biography is to inspire, not merely inform. This being the case, a question remains: What does it mean to us that these composers shared a common faith in God?

In part, the answer must be a personal one. To me, it is a great encouragement to learn about the faith of noted composers who lived years before me. As I researched this work, I felt challenged by Ives' unselfishness and Beethoven's determination. Similarly, seeking to unravel the mysteries of Liszt's faith and Wagner's jumbled belief system deepened my understanding of how Christian faith relates to everyday life.

Beyond my own personal journey of discovery about these composers, however, I believe there are other compelling reasons for learning about their faith. To begin with, after studying not only these twenty men, but also the lives of dozens of other great composers, I have discovered an unmistakably high degree of belief. The composers selected for this book were certainly not the only masters with spiritual convictions—far from it. It could have contained Vivaldi, Schumann, Palestrina, Tchaikovsky, Corelli, Rimsky-Korsakov, Massenet, or many others. There are, of course, some exceptions, but not as many as you might think.

What I conclude, based on a large amount of biographical evidence, is that the composers are, as a group, surprisingly and often deeply religious. Even those with the most secular lifestyles always seem to have a sincere respect for the Deity—a hunger for something greater than themselves which transcends everyday existence.

Why is this the case? Is it an extra sensitivity? Does it arise out of an almost god-like compulsion within a composer to create something that previously did not exist? I am reminded of something once said by Albert Einstein, a genius from another field of creativity: "The more I study physics, the more I'm drawn to metaphysics." Perhaps composers and creative geniuses detect spiritual realities to which others are generally unaware.

The sensitivity of these masters led them to a common conclusion, summarized by Beethoven: "It was not a fortuitous meeting of chordal atoms that made the world; if order and beauty are reflected in the constitution of the universe, then there is a God." These composers, who always realize that their most appreciative audiences will appear long after their death, were seldom satisfied with the superficiality and materialism of this life.

Their faith throughout the ages cannot help but suggest that Christian experience is authentic, that it is based on verifiable evidence, and that it finds expression in a wide variety of ways.

Remember the words of Stravinsky, when asked about his conversion to Christianity in his forties? The composer did not mention the actions of theologians or denominations, he said he was convinced by "a reading of the Gospels." He went directly to the source—to Jesus' original teachings: that God loves all men, that mankind is fallen and in need of redemption, that Jesus Christ died on a cross to pay the penalty for man's sins, and that we must believe in Christ and his sacrifice for us to obtain salvation. It was here that the composer found the truth upon which he could base his life.

All too often we tend to associate, and even equate religion with this-or-that church, movement, or denomination. Yet Bach himself, perhaps the most conventional churchman of this book, believed quite a mix of doctrines that no single church contained. The basis for these composers' beliefs was not an external structure, but an internal, personal relationship between each of them and Christ. Their faith grew, not by mere acquiescence to what they were taught by their parents or their church leaders, but by deep soul-searching, groping, and determination to discern the truth for themselves.

The very diversity of authentic Christian belief displayed by these composers also challenges me not to condemn other Christians who do not believe precisely as I do. It is so easy to fall into the error of judging those who attend different churches, adhere to different denominations, or even worship in different styles. Not only did these twenty composers come from a wide variety of denominations, but each of them respected Christians from dissimilar backgrounds.

Finally, a point might be made against criticisms and our present-day viewpoint of the faults of these very human composers. Once, after lecturing on Mozart's faith, a fellow Christian remonstrated with me over the small set of letters that the composer wrote as a youth which are rife with profanity. Rather than trying to defend Mozart for what was obviously profane, I found myself asking, "Would you want everything you've ever written or said to be published and studied by posterity?"

It never hurts to be reminded that our "biographers" are indeed all around us—they are the ones who observe our daily lives, feel the influence of our words, actions and emotions. The fact of our intense interest in the lives of composers who lived centuries before us provides a sobering reminder: Do we live with integrity, lives that are consistent with our beliefs?

After spending years scrutinizing these composers' lives to find what they believed, I am left with the serious question for myself, and for all of us: "If a biographer should someday research my life, what tangible verifications of my faith would be evident?" Perhaps the greatest lesson we can learn from these musicians, both in failure and success, involves the value of self-examination in light of what we understand about God.

These composers experienced a personal faith in a loving God, who gave their lives purpose. They recognized that their musical talents were a gift from God, and they determined to use these gifts to the utmost. As we have seen, they were not men without problems; and in some cases their troubles were at least

partly self-imposed. But their faith in God enabled them to prevail despite their difficulties, and to create masterpieces that have
enriched the lives of many generations. Understanding their faith
augments our appreciation of their music and their individuality,
and it brings us back again to a personal response.

The experience of Christianity is meant for all times. A common thread of faith links each of these composers whose lives span
three centuries. Fortunately, their spiritual experiences continue
to be available to us today. Their faith has inspired my faith, and I
hope it has inspired yours as well.

About the Author

Patrick Kavanaugh is well known as a composer, conductor, lecturer, and as the Executive Director of the Christian Performing Artists' Fellowship. As the conductor of the Asaph Ensemble, he has performed at many of America's finest concert halls, and in 1993 became the first American invited to conduct opera at Moscow's Bolshoi Theatre. He is the author of four books: *The Spiritual Lives of Great Composers, Raising Musical Kids, Spiritual Moments with the Great Composers,* and *Music of the Great Composers.* He has lectured extensively on the subject of the spiritual lives of great composers at universities, churches, the National Portrait Gallery, and the State Department.

Born in Nashville, Tennessee in 1954, Kavanaugh's musical education includes a Bachelor of Music from the CUA School of Music, a Master of Music, and a Doctor of Musical Arts, both from the University of Maryland, where he served for three years as a Graduate Fellow. He has also done extensive postdoctoral work in musicology, music theory, and conducting. His teachers have included Conrad Bernier, Mark Wilson, George Thaddeus Jones, and Lloyd Geisler.

As a composer, he currently has eighteen compositions published by Carl Fischer, Inc., licensed by Broadcast Music, Inc. (BMI). Kavanaugh has composed in a wide variety of genre, from orchestral to chamber music, from opera to electronic music. Larger works include his opera: *The Last Supper;* a ballet: *The Song of Songs;* and orchestral pieces: *Jack in the Beanstalk* (for 148 musicians, all on separate parts); *Three Poems of George Herbert;* and *Prelude to the Last Letter of John Keats.* His many chamber compositions include fourteen solo pieces (the Debussy Variations series), five quartets, the *New Testament Suite*, *The Art of the Maze*, and the *Homage to C. S. Lewis*. His many performances include such unusual works as the *Symphonic Parade* (premiered in the middle of Wisconsin Avenue in Georgetown), *Jubal* (for "self-accompanied" soprano), and *Music of the Spheres*, which received extensive national attention in 1975.

The favorable response to his work has been remarkable. "Dr. Patrick Kavanaugh offered a spectacular performance," claims the *Courier*, and the *Uptown Citizen* called him, "a gifted man, whose love and joy in his work are evident." The *Washington Post* notes that "His goal in creating this unusual concept is to take contemporary (classical) music out of just the conservatory and get it out to a large scale public," while *Accent* magazine praises Kavanaugh's music as, "an attempt to meet the musical public on its own ground." One astonished editor declared that, "Attempting to explain Patrick Kavanaugh's compositions is comparable to delivering a precise and simplified explanation of nuclear theory." The *Journal* newpapers commented, "A bust of Kavanaugh? Well, not quite yet, but judging from the young composer's progress, the first early motions have already been chipped into expression."

Dr. Kavanaugh now serves full-time as the Executive Director of the Christian Performing Artists' Fellowship. He resides near Washington, D.C., with his wife, Barbara, and their four children.

About the Christian Performing Artists' Fellowship

The Christian Performing Artists' Fellowship (CPAF) is a classical music and dance ministry dedicated to performing classical music to the glory of God and to spreading the Gospel of Jesus Christ. Begun in 1984, it has attracted over 700 Christian musicians and dancers to its ranks.

Dr. Richard Halverson, former Chaplain to the United States Senate, wrote after a CPAF performance, "It was outstanding. The orchestra, chorus and soloists—all believers—were of the highest professional calibre. The dance troupe and choreography were inspiring, exalting the Lord and his glory." *Christianity Today* notes that CPAF, "strives to bring the Gospel to a relatively overlooked group: the secular arts world." The *National Christian Reporter* calls CPAF members "missionaries," who are "all dedicated to bringing the Gospel of Christ to those who might otherwise not hear it."

As a unique Christian ministry, CPAF members have performed for thousands in some of the most noted halls in the Washington, D.C. area including the Kennedy Center Concert Hall, the Lisner Auditorium, Constitution Hall, Alden Theatre, Gaston Hall, and the National Portrait Gallery. CPAF performers—instrumentalists, singers, and dancers—come from over 500 churches and some 50 different denominations.

CPAF has performed and choreographed such major works as Mozart's *Requiem*, the Bach *Magnificat* and *B Minor Mass*, Stravinsky's *Symphony of Psalms*, the Brahms *Requiem*, and in 1989 the premiere of an acclaimed annual event in Washington: CPAF's choreographed version of Handel's *Messiah*. In 1991, CPAF presented its first opera production at the Kennedy Center, featuring Metropolitan Opera star Jerome Hines in the title role of Boito's *Mefistofele*. In the summer of 1993, CPAF made its international debut at Moscow's Bolshoi Theatre, where it presented Hines' opera, *I Am the Way*, based on the life of Jesus Christ. The production was shown on national television throughout Russia. Many CPAF performing groups called Selah Ensembles (String Quartet, Woodwind Quintet, Brass Quintet, Dance Troupe, and others) now perform throughout the Washington, D.C. area, and chapters are being established in other cities. The largest CPAF group, the Asaph Ensemble (named after King David's chief musician), consists of combining a large orchestra, chorus, and dance company.

CPAF is now sponsoring an annual summer project: the MasterWorks Festival. They have assembled a distinguished faculty of some of the greatest Christian performers and teachers who will come together each summer in western New York. Their purpose is to create an excellent learning environment for the exceptional college and high school students who will be the performers of tormorrow.

All CPAF performances are free of charge so that no one is hindered from hearing the performance or the message for lack of funds. All expenses, including hall rentals, printing, publicity, and mailing, are met by donations, given by individuals who appreciate CPAF's unique ministry. The Christian Performing Artists' Fellowship is a registered nonprofit, tax-exempt organization. For more information on CPAF call (703) 385-CPAF.

The Christian Performing Artists' Fellowship
10523 Main Street, Suite 31
Fairfax, Virginia 22030

e-mail: cpaf@dcez.com
home page: http://www.dcez.com/~cpaf/cpaf.htm

Notes

Chapter 1—Johann Sebastian Bach

1. Johann Nikolaus Forkel, *Johann Sebastian Bach, His Life, His Art, and Work* (New York: Da Capo, 1970), 106.

2. Sedley Taylor, *Life of J. S. Bach: Church Musician and Composer* (Cambridge: MacMillan & Bowes, 1897), 52.

3. Robert W. S. Mendl, *The Divine Quest in Music* (New York: Philosophical Library, 1957), 59.

4. Friedrich Blume, *Two Centuries of Bach, an Account of Changing Tastes* (London: Oxford University Press, 1950), 14.

5. Max Hinrichen, *Hinrichen's Musical Year Book*, vol. 7 (London: Hinrichen Editions Ltd., 1952), 263.

6. Albert Schweitzer, *J. S. Bach* (New York: Dover Publications, 1911), 166–7.

7. Paul Hindemith, *Johann Sebastian Bach, Heritage and Obligation* (New Haven: Yale University Press, 1952), 35.

8. Charles Hubert Hasting Perry, *J. S. Bach—The Story of the Development of a Great Personality* (Westport, Conn.: Greenwood, 1970), 533.

9. Hans Theodore David and Arthur Mendel, *The Bach Reader* (New York: W. W. Norton & Company, 1966), 24.

10. Ibid., 60, 67, 92, 111, 115, 125, 128, 151, 160.

11. Karl Geiringer, *Johann Sebastian Bach, Culmination of an Era* (New York: Oxford University Press, 1966), 87.

12. Wilibald Gurlitt, *Johann Sebastian Bach, the Master and His Work* (St. Louis: Concordia, 1957), 12.

13. David and Mendel, *The Bach Reader*, 98.

14. Charles Sanford Terry, *The Music of Bach, an Introduction* (New York: Dover Publications, 1963), 17.

15. Gerhard Herz, "Bach's Religion," *Journal of Renaissance and Baroque Music* 1, no. 2 (June 1946): 126.

16. Wilfrid Mellers, *Bach and the Dance of God* (New York: Da Capo, 1981), 155.

17. Herz, "Bach's Religion," 132–33.

18. Robin Leaver, *J. S. Bach As Preacher* (St. Louis: Concordia, 1982), 13.

19. Ibid.

20. Ibid.

21. Leo Schrade, "Bach: The Conflict Between the Sacred and the Secular," *Journal of the History of Ideas* 7, no. 2 (New York, College of the City of New York, April 1946): 166.

22. Paul Frederick Foelber, *Bach's Treatment of the Subject of Death in His Choral Music* (St. Louis: Concordia, 1961), 7.

23. Herz, "Bach's Religion, 135.

24. Paul Sauer, *The Life-Work of J. S. Bach* (St. Louis: Concordia, 1929), 6.

25. Philipp Spitta, *Johann Sebastian Bach* (New York: Dover Publications, 1951), 275.

Chapter 2—George Frédéric Handel

1. Richard D. Dinwiddie, "Messiah, Behind the Scenes of Handel's Masterpiece," *Christianity Today* (Dec. 17, 1982), 16.

2. John Allanson Benson, *Handel's Messiah, the Oratorio and Its History* (London: Reeves, 1897), 2.

3. Watkins Shaw, *A Textual and Historical Companion to Handel's Messiah* (Borough Green: Novello, Ltd., 1965), 24.

4. Newman Flower, *Handel, His Personality and His Times* (London: Panther Books, Ltd., 1919), 272.

5. Ibid., 272.

6. Robert Manson Myers, *Handel's Messiah, a Touchstone of Taste* (New York: Octagon Books, 1971), 63.

7. Hertha Pauli, *Handel and the Messiah Story* (New York: Meredith, 1968), 51.

8. Charles Hazilip Webb, *Handel's Messiah: A Conductor's View* (Bloomington: Indiana University Press, 1978), 4.

9. Robert Manson Myers, *Early Criticism of Handelian Oratorio* (Williamsburg: Manson Park Press, 1947), 18.

10. John Mainwaring, *Memoirs of the Life of George Frideric Handel* (London: Dodsley, 1860), 136.

11. A. E. Bray, *Handel, His Life, Personal and Professional* (London: Ward & Company, 1857), 63.

12. Percy M. Young, *The Oratorios of Handel* (London: Dobson, Ltd., 1949), 100.

13. Myers, *Handel's Messiah*, 238.

14. John Tobin, *Handel's Messiah, A Critical Account of the Manuscript Sources and Printed Editions* (New York: St. Martins Press, Inc., 1969), 161.

15. William Coxe, *Anecdotes of George Frideric Handel and John Christopher Smith* (London: Bulmer, 1799), 29.

16. Myers, *Handel's Messiah*, 80.

17. Winton Dean, *Handel* (New York: W. W. Norton & Company, 1980), 74.

18. Myers, *Handel's Messiah*, 79–80.

19. Erich H. Muller, *The Letters and Writings of George Frideric Handel* (Freeport: Books for Libraries Press, 1970), 86.

20. Paul Henry Lang, *George Frideric Handel* (New York: W. W. Norton & Company, 1966), 104.

21. Tobin, *Handel's Messiah*, 161.

22. Robert Turnbull, *Musical Genius and Religion* (London: S. Wellwood Publishers, 1907), 27.

23. Otto Erich Deutsch, *Handel, A Documentary Biography* (London: Adam & Charles Black, 1955), 819.

24. Flower, *Handel, His Personality*, 333.

25. Dinwiddie, "Messiah, Behind the Scenes," 19.

Chapter 3—Franz Joseph Haydn

1. Rosemary Hughes, *Haydn* (London: J. M. Dent & Sons Ltd., 1966), 4.

2. Ibid., 5.

3. Ibid., 18.

4. George August Griesinger, *Biographical Notes Concerning Joseph Haydn* (Madison: University of Wisconsin Press, 1963), 56.

5. Hughes, *Haydn*, 47.

6. Christina Stadtlaender, *Joseph Haydn of Eisenstadt* (London: Dennis Dobson, 1968), 66.

7. Albert Christoph Dies, *Biographical Accounts of Joseph Haydn* (Madison: University of Wisconsin Press, 1963), 139.

8. Heinrich Edward Jacob, *Joseph Haydn, His Art, Times and Glory* (Westport, Conn.: Greenwood, 1950), 273.

9. Brian Redfern, *Haydn, a Biography* (Hamden, Conn.: Archon, 1970), 35.

10. Jacob, *Joseph Haydn, His Art*, 272.

11. Ibid., 272–73.

12. Ludwig Nohl, *The Life of Haydn* (St. Clair Shores, Mich.: Scholarly, 1970), 168.

13. Marion M. Scott, "Haydn: Relics and Reminiscences in England," *Music and Letter*, 13, no. 2, (April 1932): 136.

14. Griesinger, *Biographical Notes*, 54.

15. Henri Beyle, *Haydn, Mozart, and Metastasio* (New York: Grossman, 1972), 149.

16. Griesinger, *Biographical Notes*, 53–54.

17. Howard Chandler Robbins Landon, *The Collected Correspondence and London Notebooks of Joseph Haydn* (Fairlawn, NJ: Essential, 1959), 187.

18. Neil Butterworth, *Haydn, His Life and Times* (Kent: Midas Books, 1977), 122.

19. Beyle, *Haydn, Mozart*, 149–50.

20. Scott, "Haydn: Relics and Reminiscences, 135–36.

21. Landon, *Haydn, Chronicle and Works* (Bloomington: Indiana University Press, 1977), 439.

22. Walter Pass, "Melodic Construction in Haydn's Two Salve Regina Settings," *Haydn Studies: Proceedings of the International Haydn Conference, 1975* (New York: W. W. Norton, 1981), 273.

23. Hurwitz, Joachim, "Haydn and the Freemasons," *The Haydn Yearbook*, vol. 16 (Bryn Mawr: Theodore Presser, 1985), 5.

24. Karl and Irene Geiringer, *Haydn, a Creative Life in Music* (Berkeley: University of California Press, 1968), 93.

25. Hughes, *Haydn*, 193.

26. Geiringer, *Haydn, a Creative Life*, 12–13.

27. Weiss Piero, *Letters of Composers Through Seven Centuries* (Philadelphia: Chilton, 1976), 115.

28. Michel Brenet, *Haydn* (New York: Benjamin Blom, 1972), 58–59.

29. James Cuthbert Hadden, *Haydn* (New York: AMS, 1977), 147.

30. Griesinger, *Haydn, a Creative Life*, 54.

31. Herbert F. Peyser, *Joseph Haydn, Servant and Master* (New York: The Philharmonic Symphony Society of New York, 1950), 50.

Chapter 4—Wolfgang Amadeus Mozart

1. Arthur Hutchings, *Mozart, the Man, the Musician* (London: Thames & Hudson, 1976), 101.

2. Friedrich Kerst, ed., *Mozart, the Man and the Artist Revealed in His Own Words*, trans. Henry Krehbiel (New York: Dover, 1965), 95.

3. Alfred Einstein, *Mozart, His Character, His Work* (London: Cassell & Co. Ltd., 1946), 78.

4. Kerst, *Mozart, the Man*, 93.

5. Ibid., 96.

6. Ibid.

7. Ludwig Nohl, *Life of Mozart* (London: Longmans, Green, and Co., 1877), 59–60.

8. Einstein, *Mozart, His Character*, 79.

9. Otto Erich Deutsch, *Mozart: A Documentary Biography* (Stanford: Stanford University Press, 1965), 540.

10. Otto Jahn, *Life of Mozart* (New York: Cooper Square, 1910), 267.

11. Paul Nettl, *Mozart and Masonry* (New York: Da Capo, 1957), 31.

12. Katherine Thomson, *The Masonic Thread in Mozart* (London: Lawrence & Wishart, 1977), 172.

13. Einstein, *Mozart, His Character*, 85.

14. Hans Mersmann, ed., *Letters of Wolfgang Amadeus Mozart* (New York: Dover, 1972), 111.

15. Kerst, *Mozart, the Man*, 96.

16. Ibid.

17. Ibid., 95.

18. Ibid., 97.

19. Ibid.

20. Walter James Turner, *Mozart, the Man and His Work* (Westport, Conn.: Greenwood, 1938), 341.

21. Jahn, *Life of Mozart*, 391–92.

22. Ibid., 391.

23. Franz Nemetschek, *The Mozart Handbook*, ed. Louis Bianciolli (Westport, Conn.: Greenwood, 1954), 146.

24. Michael Levey, *The Life and Death of Mozart* (London: Cardinal, 1971), 268.

25. Emily Anderson, ed., *The Letters of Mozart and His Family* (New York: St. Martins, 1966), 557.

Chapter 5—Ludwig van Beethoven

1. Michael Hamburger, *Beethoven, Letters, Journals, and Conversations* (Gordon City: Doubleday, 1960), 32.

2. Ibid., 31–32.

3. Ates Orga, *Beethoven, His Life and Times* (Neptune City, NJ: Paganiniana, 1980), 135.

4. Maynard Solomon, *Beethoven Essays* (Cambridge: Harvard University Press, 1988), 218.

5. Robert W. S. Mendl, *The Divine Quest in Music* (New York: Philosophical Library, 1957), 86.

6. Ibid., 86–87.

7. Howard Chandler Robbins Langdon, *Beethoven: A Documentary Study* (New York: MacMillan, 1970), 205–6.

8. Elliott Forbes, *Thayer's Life of Beethoven* (Princeton: Princeton University Press, 1973), 482.

9. Anton Felix Schindler, *Beethoven As I Knew Him* (London: Faber & Faber, 1966), 365.

10. James Burnett, *Beethoven and Human Destiny* (New York: Roy, 1966), 19.

11. Solomon, *Beethoven Essays*, 216.

12. Ibid., 216–17.

13. Friedrich Kerst, *Beethoven, the Man and the Artist, As Revealed in His Own Words* (New York: Dover, 1964), 104.

14. Solomon, *Beethoven Essays*, 223.

15. Ibid.

16. Mendl, *The Divine Quest*, 87.

17. Kerst, *Beethoven, the Man*, 106.

18. Philip Kruseman, *Beethoven's Own Words* (London: Hinricksen Edition, 1947), 53.

19. Ibid.

20. George R. Marek, *Beethoven, Biography of a Genius* (London: William Kimber, 1969), 177.

21. Mendl, *The Divine Quest*, 86.

22. Marek, *Beethoven, Biography*, 177.

23. Solomon, *Beethoven Essays*, 220–21.

24. Ibid., 228.

25. Hugh Reginald Haweis, *Music and Morals,* (New York: Harper, 1900), 85–86.

26. Alan Tyson, "The 1803 Version of Beethoven's *Christus am Oelberge*," *The Musical Quarterly* 56, no. 4 (October 1970): 551.

27. Solomon, *Beethoven Essays*, 220.

28. Ibid., 218–19.

29. Joseph De Marliave, *Beethoven's Quartets* (New York: Dover, 1961), 328.

30. Paul Miles, *Beethoven's Sketches* (New York: Dover, 1974), 154.

31. Warren Kirkendale, "New Roads to Old Ideas in Beethoven's Missa Solemnis," *The Musical Quarterly* 56, no. 4 (October 1970): 676.

32. George Grove, *Beethoven and His Nine Symphonies* (New York: Dover, 1962), 326.

33. Marek, *Beethoven, Biography*, 179.

34. Mendl, *The Divine Quest*, 91.

35. J. W. N. Sullivan, *Beethoven, His Spiritual Development* (New York: Mentor, 1927), 118.

36. Mendl, *The Divine Quest*, 93

37. Wilfred Mellers, *Beethoven and the Voice of God* (New York: Oxford University Press, 1983), 3.

38. Marek, *Beethoven, Biography*, 560.

39. John N. Burk, *The Life and Works of Beethoven* (New York: Random House, 1943), 206.

40. Marek, *Beethoven, Biography*, 561.

41. Irving Kolodin, *The Interior Beethoven* (New York: Alfred A. Knopf, 1975), 268.

Chapter 6—Franz Peter Schubert

1. Otto Erich Deutsch, *Schubert, Memoirs of His Friends* (London: Adam & Charles Black, Ltd., 1958), 184–85.

2. George Lowell Austin, *The Life of Franz Schubert* (Boston: Shepard & Gill, 1873), 10.

3. Deutsch, *Schubert, Memoirs*, 52.

4. Otto Erich Deutsch, *Schubert: A Documentary Biography* (New York: Da Capo, 1977), 822–23.

5. Maurice J. E. Brown, *Schubert, a Critical Biography* (New York: St. Martin's, 1958), 13.

6. Robert Haven Schauffler, *Franz Schubert, the Ariel of Music* (New York: G. P. Putnam's Sons, 1949), 27.

7. Deutsch, *Schubert, Memoirs*, 57.

8. Ibid., 184.

9. Heinrich Kreissle Von Hellborn, *The Life of Franz Schubert*, vol. 1 (New York: Vienna, 1972), 12.

10. Deutsch, *Schubert: A Documentary*, 571.

11. Ibid., 572.

12. Newman Flower, *Franz Schubert* (London: Cassell & Company, Ltd., 1928), 24.

13. Otto Erich Deutsch, ed., *Franz Schubert's Letters and Other Writings* (London: Faber & Gwyer, Ltd., 1928), 29.

14. Karl Kobald, *Franz Schubert and His Times* (London: Kennikat, 1928), 112.

15. Ralph Bates, *Franz Schubert* (Edinburgh: Peter Davies, Ltd., 1934), 76.

16. Flower, *Franz Schubert*, 53.

17. Alfred Einstein, *Schubert, a Musical Biography* (New York: Oxford University Press, 1951), 312–13.

18. Peggy Woodford, *Schubert, His Life and Times* (Kent: Midas, 1978), 135.

19. Ibid., 134.

20. Carl A. Abram, *The Music of Schubert*, ed. Gerald Abraham (New York: N. N. Norton, 1947), 225–26.

21. Oskar Bie, *Schubert, The Man* (Westport, Conn.: Greenwood, 1971), 192.

22. Dietrich Fischer-Dieskau, *Schubert, a Biographical Study of His Songs* (London: Cassell & Company, Ltd., 1971), 127.

23. John Reed, *Schubert, the Final Years* (London: Faber & Faber, Ltd., 1972), 239.

24. Maurice J. E. Brown, *Essays on Schubert* (New York: St. Martin's, 1966), 124.

25. Reed, *Schubert, the Final Years*, 219.

26. Austin, *The Life of Franz Schubert*, 51–52.

27. Reed, *Schubert, the Final Years*, 239.

28. Deutsch, *Schubert: A Documentary*, 598.

29. Reed, *Schubert, the Final Years*, 239.

Chapter 7—Felix Mendelssohn

1. Ferdinand Hiller, *Mendelssohn, Letters and Recollections* (New York: Vienna, l972), 84.

2. Eric Werner, *Mendelssohn: A New Image of the Composer and His Age* (London: Collier-MacMillan, Ltd., 1963), 38.

3. Ibid., 37.

4. Sebastian Hensel, *The Mendelssohn Family: From Letters and Journals*, vol. 7 (Westport, Conn.: Greenwood, 1968), 74.

5. Werner, *Mendelssohn*, 37.

6. Ibid., 42.

7. George R. Marek, *Gentle Genius, the Story of Felix Mendelssohn* (New York: Funk & Wagnalls, 1972), 103.

8. Werner, *Mendelssohn*, 43–44.

9. Ibid., 208.

10. Schima Kaufman, *Mendelssohn, "A Second Elijah"* (Westport, Conn.: Greenwood, l962), 87.

11. Herbert Kupferberg, *The Mendelssohns; Three Generations of Genius* (New York: Charles Scribner's Sons, 1972), 130.

12. Gerald Hendrie, *Mendelssohn's Rediscovery of Bach* (Buckinghamshire: The Open University Press, 1971), 27.

13. Kupferberg, *The Mendelssohns*, 146.

14. Edward Devrient, *My Recollections of Felix Mendelssohn-Bartholdy* (New York: Vienna House, 1972), 302.

15. Philip Radcliffe, *Mendelssohn* (London: J. M. Dent & Sons, Ltd., 1967), 36.

16. Marek, *Gentle Genius*, 257.

17. Heinrich Edward Jacob, *Felix Mendelssohn and His Times* (Englewood Cliffs, NJ: Prentice-Hall, 1963), 220.

18. Elise Polko, *Reminiscences of Felix Mendelssohn-Bartholdy* (New York: Leypoldt & Holt, 1869), 115–16.

19. Frederick George Edwards, *The History of Mendelssohn's Oratorio "Elijah"* (London: Novello, Ewer, 1896), 13.

20. W. F. Alexander, ed., *Selected Letters of Mendelssohn* (London: Swan Sonnenschein, 1894), 96.

21. Werner, *Mendelssohn*, 42.

22. Hensel, *The Mendelssohn Family*, 337.

23. Paul Mendelssohn, *Letters of Felix Mendelssohn-Bartholdy from 1833 to 1847* (Freeport, NY: Books for Libraries, 1970), 383.

24. Hiller, *Mendelssohn*, 85.

25. Jacob, *Felix Mendelssohn*, 216.

26. Werner, *Mendelssohn*, 283.

27. Jacob, *Felix Mendelssohn*, 216.

28. Ibid., 91.

29. Werner, *Mendelssohn*, 63.

30. Ibid., 147.

31. Kaufman, *Mendelssohn*, "A Second Elijah," 304.

Chapter 8—Frédéric Chopin

1. Matteo Glinski, *Chopin the Unknown* (Windsor, Canada: Assumption University of the Windsor Press, 1955), 43.

2. Bernard Gavoty, *Frederic Chopin*, trans. Martin Sokolinsky (New York: Charles Scribner and Sons, 1977), 46.

3. George R. Marek, *Chopin* (New York: Harper and Row, 1978), 9.

4. Casimir Wierzynski, *The Life and Death of Chopin* (London: Cassell and Co. Ltd., 1951), 40.

5. James Huneker, *Chopin: The Man and His Music* (New York: Dover, 1966), 47.

6. Andre Gide, "Fragments from Journal," from *Notes on Chopin*, (Westport Conn.: Greenwood, 1949), 63.

7. Glinski, *Chopin the Unknown*, 31.

8. Ibid.

9. Gavoty, *Frederic Chopin*, 242.

10. Marek, *Chopin*, 163.

11. Glimski, *Chopin the Unknown*, 46.

12. Ibid., 35.

13. Alfred Cortot, *In Search of Chopin* (New York: Abelard, 1952), 208.

14. Moritz Karasowski, *Frederic Chopin, His Life and Letters* (Westport, Conn.: Greenwood, 1970), 378–79.

15. Gavoty, *Frederic Chopin*, 242.

16. Franz Liszt, *Life of Chopin*, translated by Martha Walker Cook (Boston: Oliver Ditson, 1953), 121.

17. Glimski, *Chopin the Unknown*, 32.

18. Ibid., 30.

19. Ates Orga, *Chopin, His Life and Times* (Kent: Midas, 1976), 131–32.

20. Adam Zamoyski, *Chopin: A Biography* (London: Collins and Sons Ltd., 1978), 279.

21. Huneker, *Chopin: The Man and His Music*, 47–48.

22. Frederick Niecks, *Frederick Chopin, As a Man and Musician* (New York: Cooper Square, 1973), 319.

23. Ibid., 320.

24. Huneker, *Chopin: The Man and His Music*, 48–49.

25. James Cuthbert Hadden, *Chopin* (London: J. M. Dent and Sons Ltd., 1934), 134.

26. Huneker, *Chopin: The Man and His Music*, 49.

27. Ibid., 49.

28. Liszt, *Life of Chopin*, 190.

29. Ibid., 49.

30. Wierzynski, *The Life and Death of Chopin*, 411.

31. Ibid., 410.

Chapter 9—Franz Liszt

1. Louis Nohl, *The Life of Liszt* (Chicago: Jansen, McClurg, 1884), 128.

2. Ann M. Lingg, *Mephisto Waltz: The Story of Franz Liszt* (New York; Henry Holt, 1951), 11.

3. Ernest Newman, *The Man Liszt* (New York: Taplinger, 1935), 29–30.

4. Raphael Ledos de Beaufort, *The Abbe Liszt, The Story of His Life* (London: Ward & Downey, 1886), 101.

5. Newman, *The Man Liszt*, 30.

6. T. Carlaw Martin, *Franz Liszt* (London: William Reeves, 1886), 13.

7. Anthony Wilkinson, *Liszt* (London: MacMillan London Ltd., 1975), 37.

8. Sacheverell Sitwell, *Liszt* (London: Cassell & Company, Ltd., 1955), 144.

9. William Wallace, *Liszt, Wagner, and the Princess* (New York: E. P. Dutton, 1927), 102.

10. Sitwell, *Liszt*, 238–39.

11. Claude Rostrand, *Liszt* (London: Calder & Boyars, 1972), 150.

12. Eleanor Perenzi, *Liszt* (London: Weidenfeld & Nicolson, 1974), 108.

13. Ibid.

14. Paul Roes, *Music, the Mystery and the Reality* (Chevy Chase, Md.: E. & M., 1955), 7.

15. Lina Ramann, *Franz Liszt, Artist and Man* (London: W. H. Allen, 1882), 384.

16. Lingg, *Mephisto Waltz*, 221.

17. Rostrand, *Liszt*, 151.

18. Bence Szabolcsi, *The Twilight of Liszt* (Boston: Crescendo, 1956), 65–66.

19. Rostrand, *Liszt*, 156–57.

20. De Beaufort, *The Abbe Liszt*, 195.

21. Lingg, *Mephisto Waltz*, 259.

22. Perenzi, *Liszt*, 104.

23. Ramann, *Franz Liszt*, 373.

24. Franz Liszt, *Letters of Franz Liszt*, ed. "La Mara," i.e., Ida Maria Lipsuis (New York: Greenwood, 1969), 14.

25. Hugh Reginald Hawais, *My Musical Memories* (New York: Funk & Wagnalls, 1884), 267.

26. Franz Liszt, *Correspondence of Wagner and Liszt*, trans. Francis Hueffer (New York: Vienna, 1973), 273.

27. Franz Liszt, *The Letters of Franz Liszt to Marie zu Sayn-Wittgenstein*, ed. Howard E. Hugo (Westport, Conn.: Greenwood, 1971), 128.

28. Ibid., 234.

29. Ibid., 144.

30. Ibid., 83.

31. James Huneker, *Franz Liszt* (New York: Charles Scribner's Sons, 1924), 98.

32. Sitwell, *Liszt*, 224.

33. Wilkinson, *Liszt*, 38.

34. Sitwell, *Liszt*, 241.

35. Janka Wohl, *Liszt: Recollections of a Compatriot* (London: Ward & Downey, 1887), 162–64.

36. Perenzi, *Liszt*, 98.

37. Wilkinson, *Liszt*, 41.

38. Ibid.

39. Ibid.

Chapter 10—Richard Wagner

1. Stewart Robb, trans., *Wagner's Ring of the Nibelung* (New York: E. P. Dutton, 1960), xxxiv.

2. Ibid., xxvi.

3. Peter Burdidge and Richard Sutton, *The Wagner Companion* (New York: Cambridge University Press, 1979), 158–59.

4. Richard Wagner, *My Life* (New York: Dodd, Mead, 1911), 23.

5. Ibid.

6. Frederick Taber Cooper, *Richard Wagner* (New York: Frederick Stokes, 1915), 188.

7. George Bird, trans., *Diary of Richard Wagner, 1865–82* (Cambridge University Press, 1980), 154.

8. Wagner, *My Life*, 469.

9. Ibid.

10. Hugh Frederick Garten, *Wagner the Dramatist* (Totowa, NJ: Rowman & Littlefield, 1977), 65–66.

11. Richard Wagner, *Jesus of Nazareth*, trans. William Ashton Ellis (St. Clair Shores, Mich.: Scholarly, 1972), 284–340.

12. Paul Bekker, *Richard Wagner, His Life in His Work* (Westport, Conn.: Greenwood, 1931), 478.

13. Wilhelm Altmann, ed., *Letters of Richard Wagner* (London: D. M. Dent & Sons, 1936), 102.

14. Robb, *Wagner's Ring*, xxxii.

15. Ernest Newman, *Wagner, As Man and Artist* (New York: Tudor, 1924), 273.

16. John Chancellos, *Wagner* (Boston: Little, Brown, 1978), 264–65.

17. Ibid., 264.

18. Ibid., 265.

19. Robb, *Wagner's Ring*, xxxv.

20. Ibid.

21. Derek Watson, *Richard Wagner, A Biography* (London: J. M. Dent & Sons Ltd., 1979), 304.

22. Robb, *Wagner's Ring*, xxxviii.

23. Bird, *Diary of Richard Wagner*, 202.

24. Robb, *Wagner's Ring*, xxxviii.

25. Ibid., xxxiv.

26. Watson, *Richard Wagner*, 304.

27. Ibid.

28. Robb, *Wagner's Ring*, xxxiv.

29. Watson, *Richard Wagner*, 301.

30. Ibid., 303.

31. H. T. Finck, *Wagner and His Works; the Story of His Life* (New York: Greenwood, 1968), 326–37.

32. Watson, *Richard Wagner*, 302.

33. Robb, *Wagner's Ring*, xxvi.

34. Ibid., xxxii.

35. Watson, *Richard Wagner*, 305–6.

36. Chancellos, *Wagner*, 272.

37. Richard Wagner, *Religion and Art*, trans. William Ashton Ellis (St. Clair Shores, Mich.: Scholarly, 1972), 233.

38. Watson, *Richard Wagner*, 302.

39. Ibid.

40. Wagner, *Religion and Art*, 231.

Chapter 11—Charles Gounod

1. Marie Anne de Bovet, *Gounod, His Life and His Works* (London: St. Dunstan's, 1891), 55.

2. Arthur Hervey, *Masters of French Music* (Plainview, N.Y.: Books for Libraries, 1976), 45.

3. James Harding, *Gounod* (London: George Allen and Unwin Ltd., 1973), 43.

4. Ibid., 44.

5. Hervey, *Masters of French Music*, 45–46.

6. Ibid., 46.

7. Robert Farquharson Sharp, *Makers of Music* (Freeport, N.Y.: Books for Libraries, 1972), 195–96.

8. Ellen Orr, *Portraits and Silhouettes of Musicians* (New York: Dodd, Mead, and Co., 1897), 213.

9. Harding, *Gounod*, 44.

10. Ibid., 43.

11. Ibid., 44.

12. Ibid., 45.

13. Ibid., 50–51.

14. Ibid., 50.

15. Ibid.

16. Ibid., 46.

17. Ibid., 54.

18. Ibid.

19. Bovet, *Gounod, His Life*, 76–77.

20. Harding, *Gounod*, 55.

21. Sharp, *Makers of Music*, 196.

22. Orr, *Portraits*, 219–20.

23. Richard Northcott, *Opera Chatter* (London: Novello and Co. Ltd., 1921), 47.

24. Ibid., 49.

25. Hervey, *Masters of French Music*, 92.

26. Vernon Blackburn, *The Fringe of an Art* (London: Unicorn, 1895), 50.

27. Norman Demuth, *Introduction to the Music of Gounod* (London: Dennis Dobson, Ltd., 1950), 44.

28. Bovet, *Gounod, His Life*, 194.

29. Hervey, *Masters of French Music*, 93.

30. Bovet, *Gounod, His Life*, 187–88.

31. Ibid., 199.

32. Charles Gounod, *Autobiographical Reminiscences*, trans. W. Hely Hutchinson (New York: Da Capo, 1970), 236.

33. Harding, *Gounod*, 222.

34. Charles Gounod, *Mozart's "Don Giovanni," A Commentary*, trans. Windeyer Clark (London: Robert Cocks, 1895), 118.

35. Bovet, *Gounod, His Life*, 219.

36. Orr, *Portraits*, 214.

37. Henry Tolhurst, *Gounod* (London: George Bell and Sons, 1904), 46.

38. Bovet, *Gounod, His Life*, 219–20.

39. Ibid., 198.

40. Hervey, *Masters of French Music*, 99.

41. Orr, *Portraits*, 215.

42. Harding, *Gounod*, 222.

Chapter 12—Cesar Franck

1. J. W. Hinton, *Cesar Franck—Some Personal Reminiscences* (London: William Reeves, 1918), 8.

2. Vincent d'Indy, *Cesar Franck*, trans. Rosa Newmarch (New York: Dover, 1910), 68.

3. Ibid., 44.

4. Leon Vallas, *Cesar Franck*, trans. Hubert Foss (Westport, Conn.: Greenwood, 1951), 251.

5. Norman Demuth, *Cesar Franck* (New York: Philosophical Library, 1949), 205.

6. Lawrence Davies, *Cesar Franck and His Circle* (London: Barrie and Jenkins, 1970), 97.

7. Demuth, *Cesar Franck*, 206.

8. Hendrik Andriessen, *Cesar Franck* (London: Sidgwick and Jackson, 1950), 15.

9. Davies, *Cesar Franck and His Circle*, 97.

10. D'Indy, *Cesar Franck*, 144.

11. Davies, *Cesar Franck and His Circle*, 98.

12. D'Indy, *Cesar Franck*, 45.

13. Demuth, *Cesar Franck*, 209.

14. D'Indy, *Cesar Franck*, 69.

Chapter 13—Anton Bruckner

1. Derek Watson, *Bruckner* (London: J. M. Dent and Sons, Ltd., 1975), 23.

2. Werner Wolff, *Anton Bruckner, Rustic Genius* (New York: Cooper Square, 1942), 104.

3. Hans Ferdinand Redlich, *Bruckner and Mahler* (London: J. M. Dent Ltd., 1955), 37.

4. Wolff, *Anton Bruckner*, 150.

5. Erwin Doernberg, *The Life and Symphonies of Anton Bruckner* (New York: Dover, 1960), 5.

6. Wolff, *Anton Bruckner*, 145.

7. Redlich, *Bruckner and Mahler*, 133.

8. Dika Newlin, *Bruckner, Mahler, Schoenberg* (New York: W. W. Norton, 1978), 65.

9. Watson, *Bruckner*, 48.

10. Wolff, *Anton Bruckner*, 151.

11. Newlin, *Bruckner, Mahler, Schoenberg*, 54.

12. Wolff, *Anton Bruckner*, 150.

13. Redlich, *Bruckner and Mahler*, 137.

14. Wolff, *Anton Bruckner*, 150.

15. Redlich, *Bruckner and Mahler*, 137.

16. Ibid., 137.

17. Paul Rosenfeld, *Musical Chronicle* (New York: Harcourt, Brace, 1923), 192.

18. Wolff, *Anton Bruckner*, 118.

19. Redlich, *Bruckner and Mahler*, 113.

20. Ibid., 111.

21. Ibid., 115.

22. Ibid., 137.

23. Doernberg, *The Life and Symphonies*, 108.

24. Natalie Bauer-Lechner, *Recollections of Gustav Mahler*, trans. Dika Newlin (London: Faber Music, 1980), 47.

25. Watson, *Bruckner*, 49.

26. Gabriel Engel, *The Life of Anton Bruckner* (New York: Roerich Museum Press, 1931), 51.

Chapter 14—Johannes Brahms

1. Walter Niemann, *Brahms* (New York: Cooper Square, 1969), 183.

2. Burnett James, *Brahms: A Critical Study* (New York: Praeger, 1972), 21.

3. Nieman, *Brahms*, 182.

4. Florence May, *The Life of Johannes Brahms* (London: William Reeves Ltd., 1911), 398.

5. Peter Latham, *Brahms* (London: J. M. Dent and Sons Ltd., 1948), 88.

6. Nieman, *Brahms*, 164.

7. Robert Haven Schauffer, *The Unknown Brahms* (Westport, Conn.: Greenwood, 1933), 210.

8. Joan Chissell, *Brahms* (London: Faber and Faber, 1977), 50.

9. Nieman, *Brahms*, 182–83.

10. Edwin Evans, *Historical, Descriptive and Analytical Account of the Entire Works of Johannes Brahms* (New York: Burt Franklin, 1912), 164.

11. John Alexander Fuller-Maitland, *Brahms* (Port Washington, N.Y.: Kennikat, 1911), 211.

12. James, *Brahms: A Critical Study*, 74.

13. Ibid., 173.

14. Schauffer, *The Unknown Brahms*, 150.

15. Arthur M. Abell, *Talks with Great Composers* (New York: Citadel, 1994), 74.

16. Ibid., 3.

17. Ibid., 5.

18. Ibid., 5–6.

19. Ibid., 11.
20. Ibid., 21.
21. Ibid., 16.
22. Ibid., 12–13.
23. Ibid., 55–56.
24. Ibid., 66.
25. Ibid., 5.
26. Ibid., 12.
27. Ibid., 20.
28. Ibid., 56.
29. Ibid., 55.
30. Ibid., 10.
31. Ibid.
32. Ibid., 22.
33. Ibid., 21–22.
34. Ibid., 17.
35. Ibid., 44.

Chapter 15—Antonin Dvořák

1. Neil Butterworth, Dvořák, His Life and Times (Kent: Midas, 1980), 15.

2. Claire Lee Purdy, Antonin Dvořák, Composer from Bohemia (New York: Julian Messner, 1950), 112.

3. Otakar Sourek, Antonin Dvořák, Letters and Reminiscences (Prague: Artia, 1954), 28–29.

4. Karel Hoffmeister, Antonin Dvořák (Westport, Conn.: Greenwood, 1970), 104–5.

5. Sourek, Antonin Dvořák, 111.

6. Mosco Carner, "The Church Music," Antonin Dvořák, His Achievement, Viktol Fischl, ed. (Westport, Conn.: Greenwood, 1970), 167–68.

7. Sourek, Antonin Dvořák, 111.

8. Paul Stefan, Anton Dvořák (New York: Da Capo, 1971), 291.

9. Sourek, Antonin Dvořák, 112.

10. Ibid., 179.

11. Ibid., 213.

12. Gervase Hughes, Dvořák, His Life and Music (London: Cassell & Co., Ltd., 1967), 171.

13. Sourek, *Antonin Dvořák*, 192–93.

14. Butterworth, *Dvořák, His Life*, 45.

15. Carner, "The Church Music," 169.

16. Jarmil Burchauser, *Antonin Dvořák* (Prague: Statni Hudebni Vydavatelstvi, 1967), 6.

17. Hughes, *Dvořák, His Life and Music*, 128.

18. Otakar Sourek, *Antonin Dvořák, The Complete Edition* (Prague: Artio, 1956), 44.

19. Vaclav Holzknect, *Antonin Dvořák* (Prague: Orbis, 1971), 64–65.

20. Carner, "The Church Music," 169.

21. Holzknect, *Antonin Dvořák*, 66.

22. Carner, "The Church Music," 166–67.

23. John Chapham, *Dvořák* (London: David & Charles, 1979), 163.

24. Sourek, *Antonin Dvořák, Letters and Reminiscences*, 195.

25. Stefan, *Anton Dvořák*, 291.

26. Ibid., 263.

27. Sourek, *Antonin Dvořák*, 112.

28. Ibid., 111–12.

29. Olga Humlova, *Antonin Dvořák* (Prague: Orbis, 1954), 25.

30. Sourek, *Antonin Dvořák*, 28.

Chapter 16—Edward Elgar

1. Percy M. Young, *Elgar, O. M., a Study of a Musician* (London: White Lion, 1973), 319.

2. Ibid., 255.

3. Michael Kennedy, *Portrait of Elgar* (London: Oxford University Press, 1968), 7.

4. Diana M. McVeagh, *Edward Elgar, His Life and Music* (London: J. M. Dent and Sons Ltd., 1955), 98.

5. Kennedy, *Portrait of Elgar*, 7.

6. Robert J. Buckley, *Sir Edward Elgar* (London: John Lane, 1910), 74.

7. Ian Parrott, *Elgar* (London: J. M. Dent and Sons Ltd., 1971), 53.

8. John F. Porte, *Elgar and His Music* (London: Sir Isaac Pitman and Sons Ltd., 1933), 43.

9. Thomas F. Dunhill, *Sir Edward Elgar* (London: Blackie and Son Ltd., 1938), 45.

10. Basil Maine, *Elgar, His Life and Works* (London: G. Bell and Sons Ltd., 1933), 104.

11. Michael Hurd, *Elgar* (London: Faber and Faber, 1969), 35.

12. Young, *Elgar, O. M., A Study of a Musician*, 317.

13. Ibid., 255.

14. Ibid., 319.

15. Parrott, *Elgar*, 53.

16. Alan J. Kirby, *Edward Elgar Centenary Sketches*, Henry Alban Chambers, ed. (London: Novello and Co. Ltd., 1957), 24–25.

17. Parrott, *Elgar*, 54.

18. Ibid., 55.

19. Jose Everard, *The Significance of Elgar* (London: Heath Cranton Ltd., 1934), 20.

20. Percy M. Young, ed., *Letters to Nimrod* (London: Dennis Dobson, 1965), 202.

21. Percy M. Young, *Letters of Edward Elgar* (London: Geoffrey Bles, 1956), 203.

22. Young, *Elgar, O. M., a Study of a Musician*, 254–55.

23. Ibid., 255.

24. McVeagh, *Edward Elgar, His Life and Music*, 97.

25. Ibid., 98.

Chapter 17—Ralph Vaughan Williams

1. Ursula Vaughan Williams, *R. V. W.—A Biography of Ralph Vaughan Williams* (London: Oxford University Press, 1964), 13.

2. Ibid., 63–64.

3. James Day, *Vaughan Williams* (London: J. M. Dent and Sons Ltd., 1961), 21.

4. Michael Kennedy, *The Works of Ralph Vaughan Williams* (London: Oxford University Press, 1964), 187.

5. Celia Newberg, *Vaughan Williams in Dorking* (Dorking: Local History Group, 1979), 32.

6. Ibid., 20–21.

7. Ibid., 20.

8. Ralph Vaughan Williams, *National Music and Other Essays* (London: Oxford University Press, 1963), 201.

9. Ibid., 175.

10. Percy Marshall Young, *Vaughan Williams* (London: Dennis Dobson Ltd., 1953), 14.

11. Williams, *R. V. W.—A Biography*, 29.

12. Williams, *National Music and Other Essays*, 175.

13. Ralph Vaughan Williams, *Heirs and Rebels* (New York: Cooper Square, 1974), 38.

14. Kennedy, *The Works of Ralph Vaughan Williams*, 316.

15. Ibid.

16. Williams, *National Music*, 226.

17. Alan Edgar Frederic Dickinson, *Vaughan Williams* (London: Faber and Faber, 1963), 31.

18. Williams, *R. V. W.—A Biography*, 183.

19. Ibid., 97.

20. Frank Howes, *The Music of Ralph Vaughan Williams* (Westport Conn.: Greenwood, 1954), 244.

21. Simona Pakenham, *Ralph Vaughan Williams, a Discovery of His Music* (London: MacMillan and Co. Ltd., 1957), 69.

22. Ibid., 68.

23. Howes, *The Music of Ralph Vaughan Williams*, 244.

24. Roy Douglas, *Working with Ralph Vaughan Williams* (London: Oxford University Press, 1972), 55.

25. Michael Hurd, *Vaughan Williams* (London: Faber and Faber, 1970), 66.

26. Pakenham, *Ralph Vaughan Williams, a Discovery*, 48.

27. Douglas, *Working with Ralph Vaughan Williams*, 55.

Chapter 18—Charles Ives

1. John Kirkpatrick, "Charles Ives," *Grove's Dictionary of Music and Musicians*, 5th ed., ed. Eric Blom (New York: St. Martin's, 1970), 503.

2. Vivian Perlis, ed., *Charles Ives Remembered: An Oral History* (New York: W. W. Norton, 1974), 76–77, 114.

3. Ibid., 112.

4. Kirkpatrick, "Charles Ives," 503.

5. Henry and Sidney Cowell, *Charles Ives and His Music* (New York: Da Capo, 1983), 30.

6. Kirkpatrick, "Charles Ives," 508.

7. Ibid., 505.

8. Ibid.

9. Ibid.

10. John Kirkpatrick, ed., *Ives: Memos* (New York: W. W. Norton, 1972), 128.

11. Wendell Clarke Kumlien, "The Sacred Choral Music of Charles Ives" (a dissertation for the University of Illinois, Urbana [Ann Arbor: Microfilms International, 1969]), 39.

12. Rosalie Sandra Perry, *Charles Ives and the American Mind* (Kent, Ohio: Kent State University Press, 1974), 79.

13. Kumlien, "The Sacred Choral Music of Charles Ives," 40.

14. Perry, *Charles Ives and the American Mind*, 77–80.

15. Kirkpatrick, "Charles Ives," 509–13.

16. Perry, *Charles Ives and the American Mind*, 75.

17. Frank R. Rossiter, *Charles Ives and His America* (New York: Liveright, 1975), 40.

18. Kirkpatrick, *Ives: Memos*, 133.

19. Cowell, *Charles Ives and His Music*, 23.

20. Rossiter, *Charles Ives and His America*, 39.

21. David Woolbridge, *From the Steeples and Mountains: A Study of Charles Ives* (New York: Alfred A. Knopf), 43.

22. Kirkpatrick, *Ives: Memos*, 133.

23. Perry, *Charles Ives and the American Mind*, 89.

24. Perlis, *Charles Ives Remembered*, 218.

25. James Peter Burkholder, *Charles Ives, the Man Behind the Ideas* (New Haven: Yale University Press, 1985), 104.

26. Perlis, *Charles Ives Remembered*, 77.

27. Ibid., 109.

28. Kirkpatrick, *Ives: Memos*, 129.

29. Perlis, *Charles Ives Remembered*, 112.

30. Ibid., 83, 114.

31. Ibid., 77.

32. H. Wiley Hitchcock & Vivian Perlis, eds., *An Ives Collection* (Urbana: University of Illinois Press, 1977), 8–9.

33. Charles Ives, *Essays Before a Sonata* (New York, Dover, 1945), 117.

34. Perlis, *Charles Ives Remembered*, 219.

Chapter 19—Igor Stravinsky

1. Igor Stravinsky and Robert Craft, *Expositions and Developments* (Garden City: Doubleday, 1962), 61–63.

2. Eric Walter White, *Stravinsky, the Composer and His Work* (Berkeley: University of California Press, 1966), 89–90.

3. Stravinsky and Craft, *Expositions*, 61.

4. Ibid., 63.

5. Ibid., 64.

6. White, *Stravinsky*, 89–90.

7. Igor Stravinsky and Robert Craft, *Dialogues and a Diary* (Garden City: Doubleday, 1962), 9. Used by permission.

8. Vera Stravinsky and Robert Craft, *Stravinsky in Pictures and Documents* (New York: Simon & Schuster, 1978), 295.

9. Roman Vlad, *Stravinsky* (New York: Oxford University Press, 1978), 157.

10. Stravinsky and Craft, *Dialogues and a Diary*, 77–78.

11. Francis Routh, *Stravinsky* (London: J. M. Dent & Sons, Ltd., 1975), 119.

12. Alexandre Tansman, *Igor Stravinsky, the Man and His Music* (New York: G. P. Putnam's Sons, 1949), 129.

13. Gilbert Amy, "Aspects of the Religious Music of Igor Stravinsky," *Confronting Stravinsky*, ed. Jann Pasler (Berkeley: University of California Press, 1986), 197.

14. Igor Stravinsky and Robert Craft, *Conversations with Igor Stravinsky* (Berkeley: University of California Press, 1958), 124.

15. Ibid., 125.

16. Igor Stravinsky and Robert Craft, *Themes and Episodes* (New York: Alfred A. Knopf, 1966), 350.

17. Stravinsky and Craft, *Expositions and Developments*, 65.

18. Neil Tierney, *The Unknown Country* (Life of Igor Stravinsky) (London: Robert Hale Ltd., 1977), 165.

19. Vlad, *Stravinsky*, 156.

20. Stravinsky and Craft, *Themes and Episodes*, 31.

21. Vlad, *Stravinsky*, 164.

22. Stravinsky and Craft, *Dialogues and a Diary*, 90.

23. Ibid., 96.

24. Ibid., 97.

25. Ibid., 25.

26. Ibid., 23.

27. Ibid., 79.

28. Robert Craft, "1949, Stravinsky's Mass, A Notebook," Igor Stravinsky, ed. Edwin Cole (New York: Duell, Sloan, & Pearce, 1949), 206.

29. Igor Stravinsky, *Poetics of Music* (Cambridge: Harvard University Press, 1947), 142.

Chapter 20—Olivier Messiaen

1. Claude Samuel, *Conversations with Olivier Messiaen* (London: Stainer and Bell, 1976), 5.

2. Almut Robler, *Contributions to the Spiritual World of Olivier Messiaen* (Duisburg: Gilles and Francke, 1986), 46.

3. Samuel, *Conversations*, 2.

4. Ibid., 102.

5. Robler, *Contributions*, 52.

6. Ibid., 97.

7. Ibid., 97.

8. Ibid., 53.

9. Ibid., 50.

10. Ibid., 96.

11. Robert Sherlaw Johnson, *Messiaen* (London: J. M. Dent and Sons Ltd., 1975), 43.

12. Stuart Waumsley, *The Organ Music of Olivier Messiaen* (Paris: Alphonse Leduc, 1975), 10.

13. Samuel, *Conversations*, 123.

14. Ibid., 3–4.

15. Ibid., 95.

16. Johnson, *Messiaen*, 47.

17. Roger Nichols, *Messiaen* (London: Oxford University Press, 1975), 29.

18. Paul Griffiths, *Olivier Messiaen and the Music of Time* (Ithaca: Cornell University Press, 1985), 24.

19. Johnson, *Messiaen*, 43.

20. Griffiths, *Olivier Messiaen*, 24.

21. Carla Huston Bell, *Olivier Messiaen* (Boston: Twayne, 1984), 8.

22. Samuel, *Conversations*, 11.

23. Robler, *Contributions*, 97.

24. Samuel, *Conversations*, 101.

25. Olivier Messiaen, *The Technique of My Musical Language* (Paris: Alphonse Leduc, 1944), 8.

Bibliography

*The major sources for each composer are identified
in the Notes. These are additional sources of reference.*

Chapter 1—Johann Sebastian Bach

Buhrman, Thomas Scott Godfrey. *Bach's Life: Chronologically As He Lived It*. New York: Organ Interests, Inc., 1935.

Cox, Howard H. *The Calov Bible of Bach*. Ann Arbor: UMI Research Press, 1985.

Dickinson, Allen Edgar Frederic. *The Art of J. S. Bach*. London: Duckworth Publishers, 1935.

Field, Lawrence. *Johann Sebastian Bach*. Minneapolis: Augsburg Publishing, 1943.

Geiringer, Karl. *The Bach Family: Seven Generations of Creative Genius*. New York: Oxford University Press, 1954.

Grew, Eva and Sidney. *Bach*. New York: McGraw-Hill Book Company, 1947.

Miles, Russell Hancock. *Johann Sebastian Bach*. Englewood Cliffs, New Jersey: Prentice-Hall, 1962.

Millar, Cynthia. *Bach and His World*. Norristown: Silver Brunett, 1980.

Newman, Werner. *Bach, A Pictorial Biography*. London: Thames & Hudson, 1961.

Rimbault, E. F. *J. S. Bach, His Life and Writings*. London: Metzler & Co., 1869.

Terry, Charles Sanford. *Bach: a Biography*. London: Oxford University Press, 1928.

Terry, Charles Sanford. *Bach, Cantatas, Oratorio, Passion, Magnificat, and Motets*. New York: Oxford University Press, 1923.

Thorne, Edward Henry. *Bach*. London: G. Bell & Sons, 1904.

Young, Percy Marshall. *The Bachs: 1500–1850*. London: Boosey & Hawks, 1970.

Chapter 2—George Frédéric Handel

Cummings, William Hayman. *Handel*. London: G. Bell & Sons, 1904.

Larsen, Jens P. *Handel's Messiah*. New York: W. W. Norton, 1972.

Rockstro, William Smith. *The Life of George Frederick Handel*. London: Macmillan & Company, 1883.

Schoelcher, Victor. *The Life of Handel*. London: Trubner & Company, 1857.

Smith, William Charles. *Concerning Handel: His Life and Works*. London: Cassell & Company, 1948.

Smith, William Charles. "George III, Handel and Mainwaring." *Musical Times* 65 (1924): 789.

_____. "Handeliana." *Music and Letters* 31 (1950): 125; 34 (1953): 11.

Streatfeild, Richard Alexander. *Handel*. London: Methuen Publishers, 1909.

Townsend, Horath. *An Account of the Visit of Handel to Dublin with Incidental Notices of His Life and Character*. Dublin: J. McGlashan Publishers, 1852.

Young, Percy Marshall. *Handel*. London: J. M. Dent Company, 1975.

Chapter 3—Franz Joseph Haydn

Gotwals, Vernon. "Joseph Haydn's Last Will and Testament." *Musical Quarterly* (1961): 331.

Hadow, William Henry. *A Creation Composer*. Freeport, New York: Books for Libraries Press, 1972.

Hocker, Gustav. *Joseph Haydn*. Chicago: A. C. McClurg & Company, 1907.

Hollis, Helen R. *The Musical Instruments of Haydn*. Washington, D.C.: Smithsonian Institution Press, 1977.

Lowens, Irving. *Haydn in America*. Detroit: College Music Society, 1979.

Olleson, Edward, "The Origin and Libbretto of Haydn's Creation." *The Haydn Yearbook*. Vol. 4. Bryn Mawr: Theodore Presser Company, 1968.

Pohl, Karl Ferdinand. *Mozart and Haydn in London*. New York: Da Capo Press, 1970.

Runciman, John F. *Haydn*. London: G. Bell and Sons, 1908.

Young, Percy Marshall. *Haydn*. New York: D. White Company, 1969.

Chapter 4—Wolfgang Amadeus Mozart

Blom, Eric. *Mozart*. London: Dent Publishers, 1975.

Blume, Friedrich. "Requiem But No Peace." *The Musical Quarterly* (April, 1961): 147.

Burk, John Naglee. *Mozart and His Music*. New York: Random House, 1959.

Davenport, Marcia. *Mozart*. New York: Scribner & Sons, 1932.

Gheon, Henri. *In Search of Mozart*. New York: Sheed & Ward, Inc., 1934.

Holmes, Edward. *The Life of Mozart*. London: Chapman & Hall, 1845.

Hussey, Dyneley. *Wolfgang Amadeus Mozart*. Westport, Conn.: Greenwood Press, 1971.

King, Alexander Hyatt. *A Biography with a Survey of Books, Editions and Recordings*. London: Oxford University Press, 1970.

Kolb, Annette. *Mozart*. London: V. Gollancz, Ltd., 1939.

Langdon, Howard Chandler Robbins. *The Mozart Companion*. New York: Oxford University Press, 1956.

Levey, Michael. *The Life and Death of Mozart*. London: Weidenfeld and Nicolson, 1971.

Novello, Vincent. *A Mozart Pilgrimage*. London: Ernst Eulenburg, Ltd., 1975.

Robertson, Alec. *Requiem, Music of Mourning and Consolation*. New York: F. A. Praeger, 1968.

Sadie, Stanley. *Mozart*. London: Calder & Boyars, 1966.

Chapter 5—Ludwig van Beethoven

Anderson, Emily. *The Letters of Beethoven*. London: St. Martin's Press, 1961.

_____. "The Text of Beethoven's Letters." *Music and Letters* 34 (1953): 192.

Arnold, Denis and Nigel Fortune, eds. *The Beethoven Companion*. London: Faber, 1971.

Crowest, Frederick James. *Beethoven*. London: J. M. Dent & Company, 1904.

Grace, Harvey. *Ludwig van Beethoven*. London: K. Paul, Trench, Trubner, & Company, Ltd., 1927.

Howes, Frank Stewart. *Beethoven*. London: Oxford University Press, 1933.

Lang, Paul Henry, ed. *The Creative World of Beethoven*. New York: W. W. Norton & Company, 1971.

Newman, Ernest. *The Unconscious Beethoven*. New York: A. A. Knopf, 1970.

Rolland, Romain. *Beethoven the Creator*. New York: Dover Publications, 1964.

Sadie, Stanley. *Beethoven*. New York: Crowell Company, 1967.

Schmidt-Gorg, Joseph. *Ludwig van Beethoven*. New York: Praeger, 1970.

Specht, Richard. *Beethoven As He Lived*. London: Macmillan & Company, Ltd., 1933.

Solomon, Maynard. "Beethoven: The Nobility Pretense." *Musical Quarterly* 61 (1975): 272.

Sonneck, Oscar George. *Beethoven Letters in America*. New York: G. Schirmer, Inc., 1927.

Chapter 6—Franz Peter Schubert

Brown, Maurice John Edwin. *Schubert's Variations*. London: St. Martin's Press, 1954.

Capell, Richard. *Schubert's Songs*. London: E. Benn Ltd., 1928.

Clutsam, George H. *Schubert*. New York: F. A. Stokes & Company, 1912.

Cone, E. T. "Schubert's Beethoven." *Musical Quarterly* 56 (1970): 779.

Deutsch, Otto Erich. "The Riddle of Schubert's Unfinished Symphony." *The Music Review* 1 (1940): 36.

Deutsch, Otto Erich. *The Schubert Reader*. New York: W. W. Norton & Company, 1947.

Duncan, Edmond Stoune. *Schubert*. London: J. M. Dent & Company, 1905.

Paine, John Knowles. *The History of Music to the Death of Schubert*. London: Ginn & Company, 1907.

Schneider, Marcel. *Schubert*. New York: Grove Press, 1959.

Chapter 7—Felix Mendelssohn

Adolf, Wilheim. *Life of Felix Mendelssohn Bartholdy*. Boston: O. Ditson & Company, 1866.

Bennett, R. Sterndale. "The Death of Mendelssohn." *Musical Quarterly* 36 (1955): 374.

Blunt, Wilfrid. *On Wings of Song: A Biography of Felix Mendelssohn*. London: Hamish Hamilton Ltd., 1974.

Hurd, Michael. *Mendelssohn*. New York: T. Y. Crowell Company, 1971.

Jenkins, David. *Mendelssohn in Scotland*. New York: Chappell, 1978.

Mendelssohn-Bartholdy, Felix, G. Seldon-Goth, eds. *Felix Mendelssohn's Letters*. New York: Vienna House, 1973.

Mendelssohn, Karl. *Mendelssohn and Goethe*. London: Macmillan & Company, 1872.

Moscheles, Felix. *Fragments of an Autobiography*. London: J. Nisbet & Company, Ltd., 1899.

Petitpierre, Jacque. *The Romance of the Mendelssohns*. London: D. Dobson, 1947.

Stratton, Stephen Samuel. *Mendelssohn*. London: J. M. Dent & Sons, Ltd., 1934.

Binck, Thomas Lindsay. *Elijah, The Story of Mendelssohn's Oratorio*. New Plymouth: Thomas Avery & Sons, Ltd., 1935.

Chapter 8—Frédéric Chopin

Bourniquel, Camille. *Chopin*, trans. by Sinclair Road. New York: Grove, 1960.

Finck, Henry Theophilus. *Chopin and Other Musical Essays*. Freeport, New York: Books for Libraries Press, 1972.

Hipkins, Edith. *How Chopin Played*. London: J. M. Dent and Sons, Ltd., 1937.

Jezewska, Zofia. *Chopin*, trans. by Krystyna Kozlowska. Warsaw: Interpress, 1980.

Jonson, George Charles Ashton. *A Handbook to Chopin's Work*. Freeport, New York: Books for Libraries Press, 1972.

Jordan, Ruth. *Nocturne; A Life of Chopin*. New York: Taplinger, 1978.

Maine, Basil. *Chopin*. New York: Macmillan, 1933.

Mizwa, Stephen Paul. *Frederic Chopin*. New York: Macmillan, 1949.

Murdock, William David. *Chopin; His Life*. London: J. Murray, 1934.

Von Lenz, Withelm. *The Great Piano Virtuosos of Our Time*. New York: Regency, 1971.

Chapter 9—Franz Liszt

Auer, Leopold. *My Long Life in Music*. New York: F. A. Stokes, 1923.

Beckett, Walter. *Liszt*. London: J. M. Dent, 1956.

Buchner, Alexandr. *Franz Liszt and His Music*. New York: John Lane Company, 1911.

Fay, Amy. *Music Study in Germany*. London: MacMillan & Co., 1886.

Habets, A., ed. *Borodin and Liszt*. New York: AMS Press, 1977.

Hill, Ralph. *Liszt*. London: Duckworth, 1936.

Seroff, Victor. *Franz Liszt*. Freeport, New York: Books For Libraries Press, 1970.

Siloti, Alexander. *My Memories of Liszt*. Edinburgh: Methven Simpson, Ltd., 1911.

Strelezki, Anton. *Personal Recollections of Chats with Liszt*. London: E. Dunajowski & Co., 1893.

Von Lenz, William. *The Great Piano Virtuosos of Our Time*. New York: Regency Press, 1971.

Chapter 10—Richard Wagner

Abraham, G. "Nietzsche's Attitude to Wagner: A Fresh View." *Music and Letters* 13 (1932): 64.

Aldrich, Richard. *A Guide to the Ring of the Nibelung*. New York: C. H. Ditson & Company, 1905.

Bennett, Joseph. *Letters from Bayreuth*. London: Novello, Ewer, 1877.

Burrell, Mary. *Richard Wagner: His Life and Works from 1813–1834*. London: 1898.

Chamberlain, Houston Stewart. *Richard Wagner*. Munich: F. Bruchmann, 1897.

Culshaw, John. *Ring Resounding*. New York: Viking Press, 1967.

Dannreuther, Edward. *Wagner and the Reform of Opera*. London: Augener & Company, 1904.

Deathridge, John. *Wagner's Rienzi*. New York: Clarendan Press, 1977.

Gal, Hans. *Richard Wagner*. London: Victor Gollancz Ltd., 1976.

Hueffer, Francis F. *Richard Wagner*. London: Chapman & Hall, Ltd., 1912.

Kufferath, Maurice. *The Parsifal of Richard Wagner*. New York: United States Book Company, 1892.

Von Westernhagen, Curt. *Wagner*. Zurich: Atlantis-Musik Buch-Verlag, 1979.

Wilson, Pearl Cleveland. *Wagner's Dramas and Greek Tragedy*. New York: Columbia University Press, 1919.

Chapter 11—Charles Gounod

Barnhill, John Basil. *Gounod's Opera "Faust."* Belfast: M'Caw, Stevenson, and Orr, 1894.

Bellaigue, Camille. *Portraits and Silhouttes of Musicians.* New York: Dodd, Mead, 1897.

Blackburn, Vernon. *The Fringe of an Art.* London: Unicorn, 1898.

Ferris, George Titus. *Great Italian and French Composers.* New York: D. Appleton, 1895.

Gounod, Charles. *Faust.* New York: F. Rullman, 1952.

Hueffer, Francis. *Musical Studies.* Edinburgh: A. and C. Black, 1880.

Northcott, Richard. *Gounod's Operas in London.* London: The Press Printers, 1918.

Stevenson, Edward Ireneaus Prime. *Long-haired Iopas.* Florence: The Italian Mail, 1927.

Wagnalls, Mabel. *Stars of the Opera.* New York: Funk and Wagnalls, 1899.

Chapter 12—Cesar Franck

Aubry, George Jean. *An Introduction to French Music.* London: C. Palmer and Hatward, 1917.

Blom, Eric. *Stepchildren of Music.* London: G. T. Foulis and Company, Ltd., 1925.

Brower, Harriette Moore. *Story-Lives of Master Musicians.* New York: Frederick A. Stokes, 1922.

Dean, Winton. *Franck.* London: Novello, 1947.

Foss, Hubert James. *The Heritage of Music.* London: Oxford University Press, 1927.

Hill, Edward Burlingame. *Modern French Music.* New York: Hougton Mifflin, 1924.

Horton, John. *Cesar Franck.* London: Oxford University Press, 1948.

Kilburn, Nicholas. *Chamber Music and Its Masters.* New York: Scribner, 1932.

Rosenfield, Paul. *Musical Chronicle*. New York: Harcourt, Brace, 1923.

Turner, Walter James. *Music and Life*. London: Methuen and Company, Ltd., 1921.

Chapter 13—Anton Bruckner

Cooke, Deryck. "Anton Bruckner," in *Grove's Dictionary of Music and Musicians*, 5th edition, Eric Blom, ed. New York: St. Martin's, 1970.

Fuller-Maitland, John Alexandria. *Masters of German Music*. London: Osgood, McIlvaine, 1894.

Kilburn, Nicholas. *Chamber Music and Its Masters*. New York: C. Scribner's Sons, 1932.

Leyrer, Max. *Anton Bruckner*. Graz: Stiasny-Verlag, 1956.

Prime-Stevenson, Edward Irenaeus. *Long-haired Iopas*. Florence: The Italian Mail, 1927.

Raynor, H. "An Approach to Anton Bruckner," in *Musical Times*, February, 1955.

Schonzeler, Hans Hubert. *Bruckner*. London: Calder and Boyars, 1970.

Simpson, Robert Wilfred Levick. *The Essence of Bruckner*. London: Gollancz, 1977.

Weber, J. F. *Bruckner*. Utica: Weber, 1971.

Weissmann, Adolf. *The Problems of Modern Music*. New York: E. P. Dutton, 1925.

Chapter 14—Johannes Brahms

Bickney, Nora, ed. *Letters from and to Joseph Joachim*. London: Macmillan, 1914.

Friedlaender, Max. *Brahms's Lieder*. Oxford: C. L. Leese, 1928.

Gal, Hans. Johannes Brahms: *His Work and Personality*, trans. by Joseph Stein. New York: Alfred A. Knopf, 1963.

Geiringer, Karl. *Brahms: His Life and Work*. London: Weidenfeld and Nicolson, 1936.

Harding, Bertita. *Concerto: The Story of Clara Schumann.* London: Harrap, 1962.

Kalbeck, Max. *Johannes Brahms: The Herzogenberg Correspondence,* trans. by Hannah Bryant. London: John Murray, 1909.

Lee, E. Markham. *Brahms: The Man and His Music.* London: Sampson Low, 1916.

Litzmann, Berthold, ed. *Letters of Clara Schumann and Johannes Brahms, 1853–96.* London: Edward Arnold, 1927.

Mellers, Wilfred. *Man and His Music: The Story of Musical Experience in the West.* London: Barrie and Rockliff, 1962.

Newman, Ernest. *From the World of Music.* London: John Calder, 1956.

Chapter 15—Antonin Dvořák

Anonymous. "How Dr. Dvořák Gives a Lesson." *New York Herald,* 14 January 1894.

Bennett, J. "The Music of Anton Dvořák." *Music and Letters* 22 (1881): 165, 236.

Chapham, John. "Dvořák and the American Indian." *The Musical Times* 107 (1966): 863.

Chapham, John. "Dvořák's Relations with Brahms and Hanslick." *Musical Quarterly* 57 (1971): 241.

Dagan, Avigdor. *Anton Dvořák: His Achievement.* Westport, CT: Greenwood Press, 1970.

Dvořák, Antonin. "Antonin Dvořák on Negro Melodies." *New York Herald,* 25 May 1893.

Fles, Barthold. *Slavonic Rhapsody.* New York: Allen, Towne, & Heath, 1948.

Kinscella, H. G. "Dvořák and Spillville: Forty Years After." *Musical America* 53 (May 25, 1993): 4.

Mason, Daniel Gregory. *From Grieg to Brahms.* New York: Macmillan Company, 1927.

Sourek, Otakar. *Anton Dvořák, His Life and Times.* New York: Philosophical Library, 1954.

Chapter 16—Edward Elgar

Anderson, William Robert. *Introduction to the Music of Elgar*. London: D. Donson, 1949.

Chambers, Herbert Arthur. *Edward Elgar; Centenary Sketches*. London: Novello, 1957.

Elgar, Edward. *A Future of English Music, and other Essays*. London: Dobson, 1968.

_____. *Falstaff; Analytical Essay by the Composer*. London; Novello, 1913.

McNaught, William. *Elgar*. London: Novello, 1947.

Moore, Jerrold Northrop. *Elgar on Record*. London: Oxford University Press, 1974.

Mundy, Simon. *Elgar, His Life and Times*. Speldhurst, England: Midas, 1980.

Newman, Ernest. *Elgar*. London: John Lane, 1920.

Powell, Dora. *Edward Elgar; Memories of a Variation*. London: Oxford University Press, 1937.

Reed, William Henry. *Elgar*. New York: Dutton, 1939.

Chapter 17—Ralph Vaughan Williams

Bergsagel, John Dagfinn. *The National Aspects of the Music of Ralph Vaughan Williams*. Ann Arbor: University Microfilms, 1957.

Even, David. *Twentieth Century Composers*. New York: Thomas Y. Cromwell, 1937.

Foss, Hubert James. *Ralph Vaughan Williams, a Study*. Westport, Conn.: Greenwood, 1974.

Illings, Robert. *Thomas Tallis and Ralph Vaughan Williams*. Adelaine: Libraries Board of Australia, 1968.

Ottaway, Hugh. *Vaughan Williams*. London: Novello, 1966.

Pakenham, Simona. *Ralph Vaughan Williams, a Discovery of His Music*. New York: St. Martin's, 1957.

Schwartz, Elliott. *The Symphonies of Ralph Vaughan Williams*. Amherst: University of Massachusetts Press, 1964.

Vaughan Williams, Ralph. *English Folk-songs*. London: J. Williams, Ltd., 1912.

_____. *Some Thoughts on Beethoven's Choral Symphony*. London: Oxford University Press, 1953.

_____. *The Making of Music*. New York: Cornell University Press, 1955.

_____, Percy Dearner, and Martin Shaw. *The Oxford Book of Carols*. London: Oxford University Press, 1928.

Chapter 18—Charles Ives

Ballantine, C. "Charles Ives and the Meaning of Quotation in Music." *Musical Quarterly* 65 (1979): 167.

Bellamann, H. "Charles Ives: The Man and His Music." *Musical Quarterly* 19 (1933):45.

Bellamann, H. "The Music of Charles Ives." *Pro Musica* Vol. 1 (1927).

Chase, G. "Composer from Connecticut." *America's Music* (1955): 653.

Copland, Aaron. "The Ives Case." *Our New Music* (1941): 149.

DeLerma, Dominique-Rene. *Charles E. Ives*. Kent OH: Kent State University Press, 1970.

Elkus, Jonathan. *Charles Ives and the American Band Tradition*. University of Exeter: American Arts Documentation Center, 1974.

Ives, Charles Edward. *Epilogue, with an Addendum*. New Haven CT: P. Boatright, 1956.

Marshall, D. "Charles Ives Quotations." *Perspectives of New Music* 6 (1968): 45.

Moor, P. "On Horseback to Heaven." *Harper's*. 197 (1948).

Sive, Helen R. *Music's Connecticut Yankee*. New York: Atheneum, 1977.

Sterne, C. "Quotation in Charles Ives' 2nd Symphony." *Music and Letters* 52 (1971): 39.

Chapter 19—Igor Stravinsky

Armitage, Merle, ed. *Igor Stravinsky*. New York: G. Schirmer, Inc., 1936.

Boretz, Benjamin and Cone, Edward, eds. *Perspectives on Schoenberg and Stravinsky*. New York: W. W. Norton & Co., 1972.

Corle, Edwin E., ed. *Igor Stravinsky*. New York: Duell, Sloan, & Pearce, 1949.

Craft, Robert. *Bravo Stravinsky*. New York: World Publishing Co., 1967.

Craft, Robert. *Stravinsky, Chronicle of a Friendship*. New York: A. A. Knopf, 1972.

Horgan, Paul. *Encounters with Stravinsky: A Personal Record*. New York: Farrar, Staus, & Giroux, 1972.

Lang, Paul Henry. *Stravinsky, a New Appraisal of His Work*. New York: W. W. Norton & Co., 1963.

Lederman, Minna. *Stravinsky in the Theatre*. New York: Da Capo Press, 1975.

Libman, Lillian. *And Music at the Close: Stravinsky's Last Years, a Personal Memoir*. New York: W. W. Norton & Co., 1972.

McCauldin, Denis. *Stravinsky*. London: Novello, 1972.

Myers, Rollo. *Introduction to the Music of Stravinsky*. London: Dobson, 1950.

Stravinsky, Igor and Robert Craft. *Memories and Commentaries*. Berkley: University of California Press, 1960.

Stravinsky, Igor and Robert Craft. *Retrospectives and Conclusions*. New York: A. A. Knopf, 1969.

White, Eric Walter. *Stravinsky: A Critical Study*. New York: Philosophical Library, 1948.

Chapter 20—Olivier Messiaen

Armfelt, Nicolas. "Emotion in the Music of Messiaen," in *Musical Times*, November 1965.

Burkat, Leonard. "Turangalila-Symphonie," in *Musical Quarterly*, April 1950.

Demuth, Norman. "Messiaen and His Organ Music," in *Musical Times*, April 1955.

Dennis, Brian. "Messiaen's *La Transfiguration*," in *Tempo*, Autumn 1970.

Drew, David. "Messiaen—a Provisional Study," in *The Score*, December 1954, September 1955, and December 1955.

Gardiner, Bennett. "Dialogues with Messiaen," in *Musical Events*, October 1967.

Gavoty, Bernard and Olivier Messiaen. "Who are you, Olivier Messiaen?" in *Tempo*, Summer 1961.

Griffiths, Paul. "Poemes and Haikai: A Note on Messiaen's Development," in *Musical Times*, September 1971.

Hold, Trevor. "Messiaen's Birds," in *Music and Letters*, April 1971.

Smalley, Roger. "Debussy and Messiaen," in *Musical Times*, February 1968.